# METAMORPHOSIS

## FROM RUST-BELT TO HIGH-TECH IN A 21ST CENTURY WORLD

Published by CelebrityPress®, Orlando, FL.

CelebrityPress® is a registered trademark.

Printed in the United States of America.

ISBN: 978-0-9991714-6-2
LCCN: 2018901605

This publication is designed to provide accurate and authoritative information with regard to the subject matter covered. It is sold with the understanding that the publisher is not engaged in rendering legal, accounting, or other professional advice. If legal advice or other expert assistance is required, the services of a competent professional should be sought. The opinions expressed by the authors in this book are not endorsed by CelebrityPress® and are the sole responsibility of the author rendering the opinion.

Most CelebrityPress® titles are available at special quantity discounts for bulk purchases for sales promotions, premiums, fundraising, and educational use. Special versions or book excerpts can also be created to fit specific needs.

For more information, please write:
CelebrityPress®
520 N. Orlando Ave, #2
Winter Park, FL 32789
or call 1.877.261.4930

Visit us online at: www.CelebrityPressPublishing.com

# METAMORPHOSIS
## FROM RUST-BELT TO HIGH-TECH IN A 21ST CENTURY WORLD

By STEVEN L. BLUE

CelebrityPress®
Winter Park, Florida

# CONTENTS

# FOREWORD

The innovation cycle is the wheel that turns our world. And it turns ever faster.

Over the last decade, the threat profile for disruption has changed entirely. We used to live in a world where CEOs worried about "bottom-up" disruption, as described by Clayton Christensen's classic, *The Innovator's Dilemma.*

Christensen identified a repeated pattern where new entrants in a market target an underserved niche with a simpler, easier to use solution and then move up market with new features over time— eventually overthrowing the complacent industry leader.

But the classics have failed to prepare companies for the digital era.

While Christensen's particular cycle of disruption has indeed repeated itself, companies today need to worry about far more avenues of disruption than Christensen's narrow focus.

For instance, Steve Jobs and Apple mastered a totally different method of disruption. Instead of going bottom-up, Jobs built products that went over the top. Products like iPods, iPads, and iPhones immediately targeted the top of their respective markets with superior products, premium price points, and then later moved downstream.

Even when confronted by a bottom-up disruptor like Android, the iPhone has maintained and even grown its dominance over the years, shrugging off Christensen's legacy model.

And new companies and entrepreneurs have followed suit with high-end entry products, including Elon Musk with Tesla and Tony Fadell with Nest.

In 2017, the threat landscape for disruption changed even more dramatically.

When Amazon bought Whole Foods, it showed the massive scale and reach of Big Tech companies like Apple, Alphabet, Amazon, and Facebook. Instead of worrying about bottom-up disruption, companies now have to worry about Big Tech swooping in and materially acquiring its way into a market.

What will Big Tech acquire next? A bank? An insurance company? What if they acquired their way into your industry?

The truth is that disruption is happening faster and with greater ease every passing year. And companies need to look out for the entire forest of disruption—not just the single tree of bottom-up disruption.

The Internet, smart phones, open source technologies, the cloud, and mega platforms like iOS and Facebook have created a fulcrum and lever arm that make it easier than ever to change the world.

It only took Mark Zuckerberg a week to code up the first version of Facebook that went viral and eventually changed the world—disrupting our social interactions and even democracy itself with filter bubbles and targeted Russian ads.

Think about that for a moment.

One coder. In college. A week.

Facebook's initial success started a digital avalanche that swept up critical resources and expertise, like Sean Parker from Napster and Peter Thiel, founding CEO of PayPal, as the first outside investor. Ultimately, the power and momentum of the platform has swept up over two billion users and changed the world.

That was over a decade ago, and it's even easier to disrupt the world today.

My career has been another example. I started out as an English major in college. For my first job, I was a high school teacher. And yet with little initial interest in entrepreneurship or technology, I've become a serial software entrepreneur, creating multi-billion dollar software products over two decades that have disrupted data management for enterprises worldwide.

For the leaders of the rust-belt economy, there has never been a more critical time to innovate. There's a simple equation at work in the world today.

**Legacy Industry + Digital Era = Digitally Refactored Industry**

Software can weave its way into any industry. Its reach and capabilities are unprecedented.

Even the highest technologies—AI, machine learning, and deep learning algorithms—have been commoditized into services that can be easily employed by anyone. If you're not arming your business with AI, you are losing ground every day you wait.

Ten years from now, the leader in your industry will be the company that best uses software, platforms, and AI services and frameworks. Let that company be yours.

There's never been an easier time to be disrupted and lose your hard-fought industry positions. Or a better time to win bigger and better markets.

While innovation is a long and arduous journey, take heart. Steve

Blue is the Steve Jobs of the rust-belt economy, and *Metamorphosis* provides a detailed map for the innovator's journey.

Jedidiah Yueh
Bestselling Author of *Disrupt or Die: What the World Needs to Learn from Silicon Valley to Survive the Digital Era*
Chairman and Founder, Delphix
Founding CEO, Avamar

# INTRODUCTION

The Doomsday Clock is ticking. . . your Doomsday Clock. . . and it only has seconds left. It is the 4th quarter with ten seconds left in the game and you're down, with no time-outs left. Your last chance is a Hail Mary pass, and the likelihood of that succeeding is only 2.5%.

If you're running a rust-belt company, the longer you wait to radically transform it, the better the odds are your last play will be a Hail Mary. . . and it will fail. As a result, your company will lose the game and go belly-up, along with your career.

This book is a wake-up call for what I call "fat, dumb, and happy CEOs", which refers to CEOs that live in "happy land" and live off the successes of yesterday. These CEOs are those who choose to deny the gathering global storm that threatens their companies in the hope they can get to retirement before that happens.

This book is also for CEOs who realize that time is closing in on them. They see the margins eroding and cheap offshore labor slowly destroying their businesses. Also, this book is for those who can see that robots and artificial intelligence are the real, true enemy of their businesses. When they face the ugly truth, they know the end is coming, unless they do something. They just don't know what to do.

If you want to know what to do, this book is for you. It provides an exact blueprint of how to avoid the coming apocalypse. However, more importantly, it shows you how to prosper in a 21st Century high-tech world.

But beware, radically transforming a rust-belt company is not for the faint of heart. It is gut-wrenching, risky, expensive, and unlike anything you have ever done before. It will scare the living daylights out of you.

I can promise you this. If you follow my blueprint, you will be successful. I know, because I've done it. And so can you.

## CHAPTER 1

# THE SCARIEST RIDE OF YOUR LIFE

When most CEOs realize their companies are going down the tubes, it is already too late. There is not enough profit left to develop new products or markets as the margins have already been squeezed too thin. Past profit, which should have been spent on the development of new products, is already gone.

CEOs are supposed to recognize threats and opportunities and mobilize resources to meet them. If this is so, then why do so many CEOs pounce on opportunities while simultaneously ignoring or denying threats? Most often, this is because opportunities conjure up happy and prosperous futures for the company, as it feels very comfortable when living in opportunity-land. However, it is much harder to mobilize resources to meet what can seem like a vague potential threat which is far out into the future. CEOs tend to deny that such long-term threats will ever materialize, with most boards and shareholders feeling the same way. This is generally because the stock market rewards short-term results that come from short-term thinking. They are quick to buy into future opportunities but choose to deny the possibility that a future threat could destroy the company. Nevertheless, future threats do destroy companies—just look at the retail sector in general, and how shopping malls are going out of business in droves.

Is it possible that nobody foresaw the rise of digital shopping? Was Amazon secretly plotting its rise under the cover of darkness? Of course not. The retail sector saw it years in advance. It just chose to deny it. In light of such a threat, the retail sector could have mobilized resources to mitigate the threat, but it chose not to. Why? Who knows. I can tell you that getting boards, shareholders, and employees to divert today's profits to prepare for tomorrow's threats is very difficult. No one wants to think about it. It is a hard "sell" because future threats are unknowable.

It is much easier to convince stakeholders to divert profit toward a happy opportunity place than to avert a dark threat. However, why can't you do both? Why can't you divert profit to avert a dark threat while at the same time steer it toward a harbor of opportunity? If your company is indeed in danger of becoming extinct, why not infuse it with brand spanking new technology? Why not totally transform it with the products and services of tomorrow?

To give one example, take a look at Miller Ingenuity's product portfolio before and after its transformation, as demonstrated below.

**BEFORE AND AFTER**

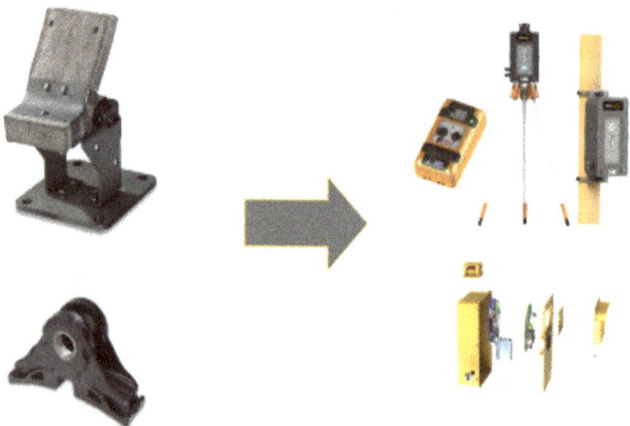

However, if you embark on such a transformation, be prepared for the scariest ride of your life; one that is full of unknowns. A ride that is thrilling and terrifying at the same time. Just when you think you are about to turn a major corner in your journey something will blow up in your face. Just when you think you have all the pieces figured out, you'll soon discover a missing piece. Just when you think the journey is complete, you'll realize it is only getting started. Such a momentous journey never really ends. It has its puts and calls, its disappointments, its surprises, its setbacks, its delights, and its soul-searching, and many times, you will wonder if you really did the right thing by starting down this road. You will find times when you wish you'd done things differently or not traveled down this road at all. Hang in there—if you made the right choice you'll know it soon enough. No matter how big they seem, you can't allow setbacks to discourage you.

Why would you want to enter the high-technology world when all you have ever known is low technology (or no technology) rust-belt products? Because the high-technology world is where all the money is. The manufacturing space is becoming increasingly sophisticated, and if you are not on that bus, you will be left behind. Sophisticated high-technology manufacturers will rule the industrial world and will only leave table scraps for those in the Rust Belt. As a result, the rust-belt businesses will go under, as they can never match the cost structure of the less developed countries.

Therefore, that fate confronts you unless you choose a radical transformation of your company. Sound intimidating and unnerving? Well, it certainly can be. In addition, if such a transformation is not handled with precise strategies, steps, and implementation, it can upend the whole company and plunge it into chaos.

It is quite necessary to disrupt a company to truly transform it, and it is quite necessary to disrupt the market to achieve profound success—anything less results in anemic growth and performance.

This section summarizes the process in terms of how it works, why it works, and how to use it. Note that there are a number of critical foundational steps to take, or the whole process will fail. The temptation to go to the back of the book and skip the foundational work will also fail. Thus, it is absolutely necessary to follow the process in the exact order stated below.

The process is truly a metamorphosis and can be comparable to how a caterpillar turns into a butterfly. Such a process doesn't happen in one fell swoop, since the process is nurtured and facilitated every step of the way.

A disruptional process needs to be structured and implemented in three major phases. Each one has to be unpacked and implemented in a certain sequence.

- Phase 1: Transform the organization from its current state into what it needs to be to move into the high-tech world.

- Phase 2: Ignite the organization's Innovational Potential™.

- Phase 3: Disrupt the market with unconventional marketing and branding strategies.

This is what your timeline will look like:

I created this process after spending 40 years in leadership positions learning what works and what does not. The process is not for the faint of heart. It will take about eight years to move through all the phases and will cost a ton of money. So you should be prepared for a long-term process. But that doesn't mean you have to make a grand announcement to your stakeholders that you are planning to fundamentally disrupt the company, that it will take eight years and cost a ton of money. That would be silly and it would only frighten them, unless you are fortunate enough to have a board that is forward-leaning and strategic. However, in my experience, I have found many boards are quite the opposite. For better or worse, many boards (and CEOs for that matter) are only concerned with the next quarter or the next year. If you preview the whole multi-year process with them, their eyes will gloss over and they won't even hear most of it. You may want to consider talking about each phase before you enter into it. You will have to make this decision depending upon the kind of board you have—just be sure not to jolt them too much or they might turn against your plan.

The foundational step that paves the way for everything else is the process of transformation. Here is the bad news—it is first and foremost a cultural transformation. If you are one of those 'gravel-and-guts-don't-talk-to-me-about-squishy-stuff' leaders you will have a hard time with this. However, it is entirely necessary. You must transform the organization from whatever it is now to what it needs to be to make the massive change from Rust-Belt to High-Technology.

What is your organization now? Knowing this is the most important step. You must understand the kind of organization you have now before you can try and transform it into something else. However, despite the fact that most CEOs think they know what their organizations are, they are often proven wrong. An example is the previous Wells Fargo CEO, who thought his organization was dedicated to "doing what's right for the customer." In spite of this claim, the organization defrauded millions of customers in the relentless pursuit of profit over a number of years.

Don't get me wrong, profit is the number one goal of a for-profit business. But how you get there and if you get there is entirely dependent on the organization's values and culture. Many CEOs think culture is all about the free beer and pizza for the lunch crowd—the squishy, feely, health and happiness types that have no place at the grown-ups table.

These days, many CEOs are beginning to understand that everything starts with culture through their realization of how the culture makes or breaks the company. For instance, consider the toxic culture at UBER, which, at the time of this writing, threatens to destroy its very existence. To give another example, the problems United Airlines has experienced through treating its customers badly—every time it gets into trouble, it reaches for a policy solution. United doesn't have a policy problem. It has a culture problem.

It is a well-known fact that super cultures produce super financial results. To achieve a super culture, you will need to install foundational core values that unleash the organization's true capability. However, be ready for the long-haul, because this cultural transformation process will take years, not months.

Ultimately, any cultural transformation should be a means to an end, not the endgame. When CEOs ask me how to do it, I always ask them, "Why?" Why do you want a cultural transformation? Well, they say, because it seems like the thing to do. I tell them they have to start with the business need. The business need has to focus on increasing profit, market share, innovation, and other business outcomes—cultural transformation is only one part of how to achieve those outcomes.

Once the organization has been transformed, it is time to ignite what I call its "Innovational Potential™." This is where you teach the organization how to be creative and where the organization learns how to unleash a blizzard of ideas. This is where you unlock the organization's inherent ability to be creative. And yes, every organization has this ability. Contrary to popular belief, most people are creative. They just don't believe they are. However, most organizations do not create environments that foster creativity for many reasons, but in my experience, they boil down to just a few.

1. The biggest roadblock is usually dumb policies and procedures that are designed for "control," not "freedom." The old command and control structure is still alive in most rust-belt companies.
2. The CEO hasn't made innovation a priority and an absolute requirement to be employed. Sure, everyone talks about innovation, but how many CEOs back that up with the time, tools, and resources to make it happen? Not many. Most organizations that start down this path ask for innovation after "the real work gets done." They don't realize that the "real work" _is_ innovation. Of course, the work that pays the bills has to get done. But innovation shouldn't be subordinated to it, and moreover, this shouldn't be an "either/ or" proposition. The so-called real work and the work of

innovation should have equal priority. Sound tough? It is, but you have to maintain the business of today while at the same time creating the business of tomorrow.

3. The compensation and incentive programs are tied to everything but innovation. This is key, because most employees will chase what they are paid to chase—and nothing else. It is crucial that innovation compensation is an equal component of other performance-based compensation programs. If you only incentivize people to get today's product out the back door, you'll never create the products of tomorrow.

Once the Innovational Potential™ is unlocked, you'll have no shortage of killer ideas and products you can bring to the market. At this point, you're almost ready to disrupt the market. But not yet. You will still need to put on some new marketing clothes.

*A key point to remember: you can't disrupt the market with killer new products if you go to market with the same tired old marketing techniques you've used in the past.*

Most rust-belt companies rely solely on trade publication advertising. You know what I mean – four-color, full-page ads that say, "we are the best" or "buy our stuff" and very little else. No one pays any attention to them and they are a complete waste of time and money. Trade publications are yesterday's marketing communication tools. You need the tools of today's digital world. And if you want to morph the company into a high-tech organization, you need to look like a high-tech company in the market.

The other tired old technique that rust-belt companies use is what I call "the blockade." You've seen this before. Have a trade show booth and make sure your linebackers block its view of the booth. Don't let anyone in that isn't one of your buddies—and they already know everything you sell.

No, if you are going to transform your entire product line to incorporate high-technology, you need to embrace the high-tech world of going to market. This requires the use of tools that include social media, digital marketing, so-called "cause marketing," video testimonials, and virtual reality demonstrations. Sound like a whole new world? It is.

It is as critical to reposition the image of your "new" company as it is to reposition its product lines. The good news is that your rust-belt competitors won't be able to predict your actions, as they will keep using the tired old tactics and by the time they figure out what you're up to, you'll be miles ahead of them. However, they won't be your competitors anymore; instead, you will be faced with new high-technology competitors and you'll need disruptive marketing. More on that in chapters twelve, thirteen, and fourteen.

***

Now that you've seen the cliff notes and outline of the book, don't be tempted to skip to the back for the answers. I wish I could say, as many books do, that you can pick and choose what interests you the most and dive into that. Unfortunately, this is not the case with this book.

A word of caution: There is great danger and great opportunity in this book. To illustrate, if you piecemeal the process, you could destroy the whole company. In addition, if you just dive into innovation without laying the transformational foundation, I guarantee you will waste a lot of money and demoralize the entire workforce. Likewise, if you transform the organization but give your employees the same old rust-belt products to work on, then you will have also wasted a lot of money; moreover, if you transform the organization and ignite its Innovational Potential$^{TM}$ without totally revamping how you go to market, you will still fail miserably.

However, I promise you, if you take this one step at a time, carefully and deliberately, you won't believe the metamorphosis that will occur. You'll witness a renaissance before your very eyes, as the organization will perform so superbly that you will stand in wonder and awe as to how they did it.

*A big mistake to avoid at all costs is allowing the transition to work on auto-pilot—rather, you must be actively involved, every single day.*

Don't make the mistake of delegating this to people below you, and what's more, don't let the health and happiness department anywhere near it—this is up close and personal, hand-to-hand combat. You need to be able to not only look into the eyes of your team but also into the eyes of your customers.

Throughout the journey, you will make a few really big decisions. However, these won't be the most important decisions you will make. The most important decisions you make will be the million little ones; for example, the day-to-day nudging, pushing, and small-course corrections necessary for success. In addition, you need to feel the pulse of the organization and the market to make the right ones.

Here is one example of what I mean. A company I ran before Miller Ingenuity was closing in on its biggest single order in its history. It was also the company's first high-tech order and would have enormous consequences for the company. Not only was the order significant in its size, but it would solidify the company's status as a high-tech leader.

Everything was wired to get the order. We had been working with the customer on it for over a year. There were enormous technical, commercial, and legal challenges to overcome to secure it. Their commercial team had already approved the order—and we were eagerly awaiting the customer's general counsel to sign off on the deal. A deadline loomed, and if it wasn't signed off by a certain date, the whole deal would evaporate. Along with it would go a year's worth of effort and significant expense. We were told the sign-off would come soon, however, the customer's legal department suddenly went radio silent. Not a good sign.

My team was waiting and hoping, which are two things that I am not particularly good at. I considered the silence on the legal end as the death knell for the order unless I did something about it. So, I would get my team together every two days and throw out ideas about how to get it jump-started. Nothing was working. But then I remembered that we had a videotaped interview from a recent trade show where the customer's CEO said he was excited that this deal was done.

Aha! He obviously didn't know his legal department was about to let the deal die. So, I sent him an email with the video and an overnight FedEx delivery with a flash drive containing the data. When I want to get someone's attention, I always use FedEx overnight delivery. People always open an overnight package because they figure it must be important. He was no exception.

Within days he sprang into action and replied that he would get the issue fixed right away, and he did. His legal department re-engaged with us within a day and the deal was done a week before the deadline. Had I not intervened with just one of a million decisions I had made on this project, the order would have been lost.

One of the most important jobs of the CEO is to find a way when everyone else has given up or run out of ideas. The CEO should never give up, as they should also be the "Idea-In-Chief". I am not saying the CEO has to have all the ideas; of course he doesn't, and neither should he. However, he should be the one that comes up with a fresh, new, original idea when it is most needed.

As one last reminder. Please don't disillusion yourself about the tough-as-nails job that this is. All your stakeholders will be against you in the beginning. Overcoming this will require all the experience and skill you've learned over your entire career. You'll have to be part salesman, part tough guy, part magician, and part motivational expert. Oh, and did I say, you'll also have to be right.

*When you set out to make a massive change, you'll be wrong...until you are right. You'll be stupid...until you're not. And believe me when I tell you, you'll be unpopular...until you are a hero.*

CHAPTER 2

# FOUNDATIONAL VALUES— RESPECT

Before you can start your metamorphosis, you need to build a strong and effective foundation for your organization. The organization policies, practices, and behaviors in the rust-belt world simply won't work in the high-tech one. Nothing short of a cultural revolution is required.

This is necessary in helping your organizational model evolve from command and control to a self-directed one. It needs to eliminate policy-driven decisions and replace them with employee-driven decisions. Further, it needs to create an environment where employees are engaged, enlightened, and energized—what I call Cirque de Soleil® cultures.

Cirque du Soleil® performers come to work every day all jazzed up to perform better today than they did yesterday. They live for their jobs, work together seamlessly as a team, and communicate perfectly with each other. Cirque performers feel valued and respected. Therefore, they want the company to be successful.

In contrast, in most rust-belt company cultures, employees drag their butts into work. They don't care if today's performance is better than yesterday's because they live for their bowling team and work in silos, without regard for the rest of the organization. Further, they withhold information from each other and don't feel valued and respected. Therefore, they are often more interested in their bowling scores than company performance.

This is not their fault. Rather, it is the leadership's fault and only the leadership can fix it. In light of this, how does leadership create a culture that is more like Cirque du Soleil® than the bowling alley? The answer is through values.

In my third book, *American Manufacturing 2.0: What Went Wrong and How To Make It Right*, I wrote extensively about the "7 Values of Ingenuity®", which is a highly integrated system for creating a Cirque-like culture by installing seven key values. These values are:

1. Respect

2. Integrity

3. Teamwork

4. Community

5. Commitment

6. Excellence

7. Innovation

Although these particular values might not be appropriate for your organization, some of them are universal and need to form a significant part of your metamorphosis. These universal values include:

- Respect

- Integrity

- Teamwork

Over the next three chapters, we will examine each one in detail. In this chapter, we will start with the most important one of all—respect.

As a leader, it is your job to create an environment of respect. Do you need grand gestures? Not necessarily. Sometimes, the simplest of respectful acts can affect morale significantly, and in turn, productivity. In a company I once took over, I noticed that some of our employees were parking their cars in the street. I thought that this was odd, so I decided to look into it. It was in the winter and the parking lot along the side of the building was on a slight slope downward toward the street.

The parking area was never paved, and was only dirt. Because of the foundation of dirt, in the icy winter, employees' cars would slide into the street. Every so often, the employees would go out and pull their cars back into the parking lot.

Apparently, the previous CEO didn't think employees were worth the minor expense of paving the lot. But I did, so I promptly had it paved. Although this was a small action, it made a real difference as it showed the employees that they were respected.

Why should you do these kinds of things? Because your competition can pay the same wages and benefits as you do. Wages and benefits are known as dissatisfiers, meaning whatever you pay, employees won't ever be satisfied. Your competition has the same dissatisfiers as you do. You can't win the dissatisfier game—but you can win the respect game.

*Respect is the foundation for business excellence.*
*Without respect, no business can excel.*

The reason many businesses languish in low margins and poor profitability is because they have cultures of disrespect, and that destroys more businesses than recessions.

I once worked for a manager who wouldn't acknowledge whether my opinion was worthwhile. I would have to guess what he was thinking, because he wouldn't tell me. I once asked him why he wouldn't comment on them, and he said, "If I tell you if it's good or bad, then I have made the decision for you, and I want you to make the decision." That was twisted logic to me, because a leader is supposed to lead, not leave his team clueless and in the dark. As a leader, you owe it to the people you lead to mentor them and give them sound advice. How else can they develop?

Leaving others in the dark on your views only breeds further suspicion that you are setting them up for a fall, or that you intend to blame them if the decision goes wrong. When people think that, as I did, it only creates mistrust between the leader and his team.

I found my former manager's approach not only counter-productive but also offensive and disrespectful. Always remember that disrespectful cultures are a breeding ground for poor performance. When leaders make people feel bad about themselves by disrespecting them, how can they perform at their best? When co-workers make each other feel bad with disrespect, how can they possibly function well as a team?

In my world, respect trumps performance every time, no matter how well a leader performs. If he treats people badly, I will give him the boot, as I have done so many times before and would not hesitate to do so again in the future.

The reason is that bad people managers will never be able to sustain good performance. When people are treated disrespectfully, one of two things occur:

1. If they are any good, they leave the company, and then you lose a star performer.

2. If they stay because they think they can't get another job, they mentally check out because of the way they are treated, or even worse, they might intentionally perform poorly, just to "get back at the boss."

Never allow a manager to treat employees disrespectfully, no matter how good his performance is. Great performance without respect is always a temporary condition. A leader earns the right for great performance from their employees as long as they are treated well; in doing so, this right is earned again the following day, with a special emphasis on "earn". Never feel as though you are "entitled" to a certain level of performance from your team— they owe you nothing; rather, you owe them. Don't ever forget that.

From a psychological point of view, respect is extremely important. We all need to be respected. It is a perfectly normal human desire to be accepted and valued by others. In the workplace, employees want to feel accepted and self-valued.

Fewer workers feel respected than most people think. According to a study conducted by Harvard Business School and Tony Schwartz[1] on 20,000 employees, half of them did not feel respected by their bosses. The researchers also stated that:

*". . . being treated with respect was more important to employees than recognition and appreciation, communicating an inspiring vision, providing useful feedback—even opportunities for learning, growth, and development. Those that did gain the respect of their leaders reported 56% better health and well-being, 1.72 times more trust and safety, 89% greater enjoyment and satisfaction with their jobs, 92% greater focus and prioritization, and 1.26 times more meaning and significance. Those who feel more respected by their leaders were also 1.1 times more likely to stay with their organizations than those that didn't."*

The researchers additionally stated:

*"Respect also had a clear impact on engagement. The more that leaders give, the higher the level of employee engagement, as demonstrated by the study, which indicated that when leaders treated their employees with respect, they were 55% more engaged."*

*Respect for the individual has a direct correlation
to the performance of the organization. As it
turns out, "nice" does contribute to profit.*

The upside is that respect results in greater performance. However, what about the downside? What happens when people don't feel respected by their leaders? According to Abraham Maslow, an author best known for his work *The Hierarchy of Needs*, the deprivation of these needs can lead to an inferiority complex, feelings of weakness and helplessness, and in addition, psychological imbalances such as depression can also occur. Doesn't sound like a healthy environment designed to stimulate high performance, does it?

When people feel weak or helpless in the workplace, they turn to people and organizations that can help them, such as labor unions, lawyers, and the Department of Justice, none of which have the best interests of your business at heart.

It is clear that leaders must respect their employees if they want high-performing organizations. However, I also contend that an organization cannot perform at its peak unless the level of respect goes beyond just how the leaders treat their employees. Every employee in the company has to be respectful of every other employee.

I once took over a business that could be considered a cesspool of disrespect. The way people treated each other was horrible. The white-collar employees had their own cafeteria because they didn't want to be around the factory employees. Factory employees didn't even have a cafeteria and weren't allowed to use the white-collar one. The language that people in the factory used with one another was closer to what might be found in a prison than in a business. I am talking about the vilest of four letter words. Sometimes the words would escalate to fights and physical abuse. It was that bad.

One thing I've learned over the years is that respect, or lack thereof, is rooted in the language people use with one another. Or more to the point, the language that the leaders permit. Therefore, the very first thing I did was to bring the entire company together and declare a zero-tolerance policy for foul language.

I first explained the fundamentals of respect to them. I told them why it was important to treat each other more like teammates than cellmates. Then, I clearly outlined the consequences of ignoring the new policy: immediate termination. No warnings, no second chances—out the door—period.

As I expected, the new policy was immediately tested. I fired a guy within hours of the announcement. The next day I fired two more. At this point, I was beginning to wonder if I would have any employees left by the end of the week! And amazingly enough, many of the employees felt I had taken away a God-given right to swear!

I stuck to my guns because I knew this was the first and most important battle to win the war for respect. If I didn't stay the course, I had no chance in creating respect as a core value in the company.

Over time, the employees who couldn't fit into a culture of respect either left or were asked to leave. Those that stayed felt much more valued and enjoyed an atmosphere of camaraderie and fulfillment. Does this sound like pie in the sky? It's not. I have seen the immense benefits that can be gained through implementing such practices.

## HOW DO YOU INSTILL A CULTURE OF RESPECT IN YOUR ORGANIZATION AND MAKE IT A CORE VALUE?

Begin by understanding that leaders should lead by example. If you are not an inherently respectful person, you don't have a chance. Therefore, leaders have to genuinely care about their employees, and moreover, they have to care about their personal lives, their hopes and dreams, their financial situation, and how they feel about the workplace. Of course, we all have bottom lines to worry about, but my experience as a leader proves that one can simultaneously care about both people and profits. After all, how can one exist without the other?

Let's assume that you are a respectful leader who cares about your people. Here is what you have to do: declare to your subordinate leaders that respect will be a cornerstone value. You need to make sure they all understand the role that respect can play in the success of the company, in addition to why it is so important, and why it *will* happen.

It is too late to change those leaders who do not treat their employees with the respect they deserve. This is because the employees already know they are jerks and one cannot simply turn a jerk into a nice guy—once a jerk, always a jerk. In light of this, organizations should plan to replace such leaders. Remember, employees always note their leader's actions and behaviors, and they will assume this is just another management fad until proven otherwise.

*Make a large part of your managerial incentive program contingent on demonstrating the value of respect.*

Evaluating respect should be a formal part of a leader's performance appraisal process. Thus, it is important to declare that respect will be a core value to the entire company. Make sure all the employees understand what respect means; don't just use the term "respect." Instead, talk about thoughtfulness, caring for each other, etc.

*Make respect a formal part of the employee appraisal process.*

This may seem a bit overwhelming, but you will not have to do this forever. You only have to do it for a while so people know you are serious about it. Put a stake in the ground that extreme disrespect is an offense that will result in termination. Otherwise, it is just a management platitude. Then, be prepared to terminate people—even star performers who violate that rule. In fact, people probably won't believe how serious you are about respect until you actually fire someone.

> *Celebrate those who demonstrate the value of respect at every chance you get.*

Reward them every chance you get.
Repeat after me: *Reward them every chance you get!*

Only after your entire organization treats each other with respect can you turn to the second foundational value of integrity.

**Chapter Bibliography**

1. Christine Porath. *Half of Employees Don't Feel Respected by Their Bosses.* Harvard Business School. *Motivating People.* November 19, 2014. https://hbr.org/2014/11/half-of-employees-dont-feel-respected-by-their-bosses.

CHAPTER 3

# FOUNDATIONAL VALUES— INTEGRITY

Merriam-Webster defines integrity, in part, as "the quality of being honest and fair," while others have defined integrity as "doing the right thing in a reliable way," or "doing the right thing even when no one is looking." To round out the common definition, there is a "steadfast adherence to a strict moral or ethical code, such as a leader with great integrity."

People with integrity are as good as their word. They do what they say, and can be relied upon to do the right thing. But "the right thing" is sometimes in the eye of the beholder. As an example, when I was in graduate school, one of the classes was *The Ethical and Legal Environment.* It was an interesting class because we examined the case studies of business situations to determine if they were both ethical and legal.

Some cases, while they were within the confines of the law, were not necessarily ethical. Conversely, while some cases were ethical, they were not necessarily legal.

A case in point is anti-trust law. Anti-trust law doesn't necessarily concern itself with the ethics of a market situation. Many anti-trust laws did not arise from ethical considerations but rather from concerns about market allocation and concentration of market power. Thus, according to these anti-trust laws, many perfectly ethical situations could very well be illegal.

Those classes heightened my awareness on the subject of ethics and integrity. Integrity is not necessarily an absolute that is clearly defined and agreed upon by all in every situation. Much like ethics and the law, integrity is more situational than absolute.

Without having a scientific test for integrity, leaders need to rely upon their common sense and personal morality. In 1964, in writing his opinion about an obscenity case, United States Supreme Court Justice Potter Stewart famously said, "I know it when I see it." When it comes to matters of integrity, most people . . . "know it when they see it." They are looking for it all around them. They are hoping to see it in their government and in their school districts. They certainly hope to see it where they work.

But what does integrity mean in an organizational setting? And why does it play such an important role in transforming an organization? These are the questions we will answer in this chapter.

I once owned a classic cherry-red 1968 Mustang convertible. Oh, how I loved that car! The first winter I had it, I needed to find a place to store it, as my garage wasn't big enough. So, I considered storing it in the company warehouse. I could do that, right? After all, I was the CEO and we had plenty of space to park the car.

The day I was supposed to bring it in, I was walking through our factory and couldn't help but notice one of the "values" banners we had hanging from the ceiling. That's when it hit me like a lightning bolt. The "Integrity" value banner jumped right out at me. It got me thinking. Even though I was the CEO, and even though the warehouse had the space to store the Mustang, was it the right thing to do? I couldn't help but ask myself, would a leader with integrity store his personal car in the company warehouse? The answer screamed out at me: "Absolutely not!"

Having been reminded of the company values, I reneged on the idea of storing my car there. However, what if I had? Would it have made a difference as far as my employees were concerned? You bet it would—employees always watch their leaders, and take their cues directly from them. Furthermore, one can't preach integrity and not practice it. In fact, if you preach any values at all, you'd better practice them yourself!

Had I stored my car in the company warehouse, people would have scratched their heads, wondering if this whole integrity thing was just a slogan or a real value that they should live by. How could I expect them to have integrity if I didn't demonstrate it? If I had stored my car there, the whole company value of integrity would have gone up in smoke.

Why is it so important for everyone in an organization to have integrity? Because integrity is the glue that binds the organization together. People can only perform at a high level if they believe in the integrity of their teammates. They have to know when they jump out of that airplane that their teammate packed their parachute properly. They have to believe when their teammate tells them something, that it is the gospel truth. Otherwise, they will always hold back, wondering if the information they received is reliable or not.

I once hired an executive who had spent years working for another company where integrity was not a high priority on their list. In fact, I don't think it was on their list at all. His previous boss would authorize him to do something only to pretend he didn't if it turned out badly. How could this executive ever confidently march into the battle if he believed the general would abandon him at the slightest hint of trouble?

Many times, I would authorize him to do something, only to have him come back to me a few days later and ask me if I was *really sure* I wanted him to do it. In the meantime, what I wanted him to do didn't get done. That resulted in missed opportunities.

Unfortunately, this story does not have a happy ending. This guy had been so conditioned to working in an integrity-free zone full of backtracking and backstabbing that he couldn't be effective.

I consider myself a compassionate leader who believes in giving everyone a fair chance. When I say I'm going to give you a chance to prove yourself, I will give you a chance. However, in business, the stakes are very high, and I can't afford to jeopardize everyone else's job simply because one person doesn't have integrity. A leader cannot bend the rules or relax the standards of integrity for one person.

I had to ask this guy to leave the company because he had no integrity. I could never trust him to pack my parachute again.

To give another example, the company was once in a competitive bidding situation and my sales executive and I disagreed on the price. He very strongly felt that I was wrong and felt he knew better.

Ultimately, he agreed to the price that I wanted. However, even though he agreed to go into the bidding process with a certain price, when he made his bid, he quoted the price that he had favored and that I had rejected.

When I found out, I was furious. As I have always said to my team, the time for debate is before we run the play. After we come out of the huddle, I expect you to run the play I called. After that incident, in my eyes he had lost all integrity and I could never again rely on him. Remember, an essential ingredient of integrity is reliability—I had no choice but to let him go.

On another occasion, we found a manufacturing employee "fudging" his production numbers. The fudges were so small you could hardly call them falsifications— here and there, he would inflate his actual production output. However, let's face it, little fudges start adding up to big fudges. If everyone in the whole factory thinks little fudges are okay, imagine the mess you would be in at the end of the month.

That employee didn't think anyone was looking. Remember that integrity is doing the right thing even when no one is looking. In fact, it is essential to believe your people are doing the right thing all the time because it is virtually impossible to be looking all the time. If your people have integrity, you don't have to constantly look over their shoulders.

What did we do about the employee who was fudging the numbers? We fired him because he had no integrity. These are tough but necessary decisions to take, as dismissing that employee sent a very clear message to everyone else about the importance of integrity. If we had simply overlooked it, we would be sending the wrong message. We would have been sending the message that "a little fudging is okay," and that integrity is not really that important.

> **When you have a high-performing team,**
> **everyone notices everything.**

If we hadn't taken actions to preserve the integrity of our workplace, we would have been on our way to becoming what I call an "integrity-free" company.

Imagine a whole company of "integrity-free" people–no one would trust anyone else, no one could be counted on to do what they said they would, and everyone would second-guess everyone else.

Can you imagine how poorly companies like this perform? Actually, you don't need to imagine it. Just read a case study of General Motors from a period stretching from the 1980s to its bankruptcy in June 2009. The story of GM, during its thirty years of decline, depicts a total loss of integrity. Executive coddling, union greed, shoddy manufacturing, lack of integrity—their history is a textbook example of how to ruin a great company.

Fortunately, GM has risen from the brink of total disaster, and this once proud American manufacturer is now regaining its stature as a global industrial leader.

## INTEGRITY-RICH COMMUNICATIONS

As a leader, one of the most important skills to hone is that of "integrity-rich" communications. This starts with total, unvarnished honesty. Some leaders are afraid to be honest with their employees because they are afraid the employees can't handle the truth, while other leaders often tell half-truths because they're afraid the whole truth might scare them, or worse yet, upset them.

So, what they do is keep their people in the dark, especially concerning matters that might adversely affect them, such as deteriorating business conditions that might cause layoffs, which is a huge mistake. People sense when things are not going well, and when you don't talk about it, they assume the worst, which is usually worse than it really is. If you don't tell them the absolute truth all the time, they won't believe anything you tell them, and if they don't believe anything you tell them, you can no longer lead them.

On the other hand, many leaders are more paternalistic and try to protect their people from bad news. I once served on the board of a university that was facing deep budget cuts that were certain to adversely affect students and faculty alike.

We were sitting around the board-meeting table discussing the best way to communicate the problem. Most of the board members took a paternalistic approach as they wanted to protect the students and faculty from the situation, and they didn't want mass defections if they found out the truth. This kind of thinking is pure folly! "These are adults," I said, "and you should treat them like adults, not like little kids. Besides, do you think they don't know this is coming? If you choose not to reveal everything you know, they will never trust you with the truth again. And once 'trust in truth' is gone, you can never get it back."

I failed to convince my fellow board members of this approach and they chose the approach of "tell half the truth and hope the other half never shows up." It is hard to estimate the credibility the board lost that day, as students and faculty alike were upset the board didn't tell them the truth.

Consider this: if you went to your doctor and had some tests done, what would you want your doctor to tell you? Would you want him or her to say, "The tests reveal you have cancer. It requires treatment. Here's how we're going to attack it. It's going to be difficult and painful, but if we work together, we can beat it." A strong, determined, and direct approach such as this one demonstrates true professional integrity.

On the other hand, this would be the half-truth way to communicate the problem: "Yes, we took some tests, and we know you have a problem, but we're not going to get into the details because we don't want to upset you. However, you need to report to the hospital immediately for surgery."

I would want my doctor to give it to me straight and help me deal with it. So do your employees. Always remember that your employees want you to have the integrity to "trust in the truth," which means to tell the truth and trust that your people can deal with it. You may very well have to help them deal with it, but deal with it they must.

If you don't tell them the truth, or if they even think you're not, they will start making things up. I guarantee you that what they make up will be worse than the truth. While they are kibitzing about a variety of disaster scenarios, how much work do you think is getting done?

But, you say, what if the truth is bad—really, really bad? If this is the case, know this: you have even more reason to be honest.

I once bought a company in Southern California. Our plan was to shut the plant down, lay off all the employees, and consolidate the business in our own facility. Naturally, my operations people were fearful that if the California employees knew of our plan, they would revolt, sabotage everything in sight, and generally make our lives miserable on their way out. It was a "really, really bad" truth.

The people in California knew we had the equipment and capacity to make the products they were making—any idiot could figure out we wouldn't want a plant thousands of miles away if we could do it ourselves. So what do you think the California people were thinking? Well, my guess is they had our plan all figured out and expected us to lie about it, or, at least, to conceal the whole truth.

Instead, we "trusted in the truth."

I had my guys put together a contingency plan for the worst scenario—all the employees walking out and sabotaging the place. I also had my human resource people put together a generous retention bonus if people stayed and cooperated until we transitioned the business to our place.

I then told the California people the ugly truth, that although I regretted the decision, I had no choice but to shut the place down. And guess what? They were astounded that I had told them the truth. When I told them about the retention package, they were very grateful for what we were doing. As a result, there were no mass walkouts or any form of sabotage; just an orderly transition.

Speaking of integrity-rich communications, what do you think our home office employees would have thought about us lying about our plan? They would certainly know we lied because they were having regular contact with the California people. You guessed it, the home office people would wonder if they could ever trust us again. They would wonder if this whole integrity thing was just a management fad.

Leaders with integrity always trust in the truth and tell people what they need to know and should know. People need to know that performance matters. If the company doesn't perform well, its future is in jeopardy. Make sure your employees understand that going out of business is a possibility. Just be sure and follow the discussion with, "But that isn't going to happen here if we all do such and such." Let them know how they can help shape their futures, and not just be victims of it. In other words, if you only tell them the bad things that can happen without giving them hope, inspiration, and the battle plan, they are bound to be scared.

Consider the flip side. Let's assume you never told your team "What could happen if . . .?" and then one day the "if" came along and you announced a massive layoff. How would you handle the following question: "Why didn't you ever tell us this could happen? If we had known, we might have worked harder, or smarter, or more as a team." This is a question that a leader should never have to answer.

Remember, the workplace isn't a Sunday School, and these aren't children. Talk to your employees like the adults they are, not like idiots who aren't smart enough to understand the world around them. The more you talk to them, and the more you talk to them with integrity, the more they will feel enabled and in control, which equates to higher performance.

In contrast, when employees don't feel enabled and in control, they spend all their time worrying about the unknown, and spend all their time trying to find ways to become enabled and in control—instead of doing their jobs.

It's not that leaders who don't "trust in truth" want to lie. More often than not they are just bad communicators; this is to say that although they may be good at the technical aspects of their job, they missed Communication 101 in college.

I occasionally find leaders who are too scared to tell the truth, such as the board members at the university. On an individual level, the board members possessed *personal* integrity; however, they didn't understand the concept of *organizational* integrity. Individually, they would have demanded straight answers from their doctors but did not understand that, as university board members, they were like doctors; their patients included every staff member, teacher, and student at the university. Every individual member of the university community deserved to know the truth.

Once you have a solid foundation of respect and integrity, it is time to implement the most important foundational value of all—teamwork.

CHAPTER 4

# FOUNDATIONAL VALUES— TEAMWORK

One of today's most overused business buzzwords is "team." Everybody talks about teams. Most business leaders talk about the need for teams, and how the organization is just one big happy team. Furthermore, few would deny that teamwork is the most effective way to optimize results.

However, if every organization were just one big happy team, why then are so many organizations dysfunctional? If teamwork is the way to go, why don't many businesses have effective teams, even though they say they want to?

Really, if teamwork is so great, why isn't everybody doing it? The answer to this question is straightforward: they're not doing it because it's *difficult*. Building and maintaining a championship team—whether you're manufacturing widgets or trying to win the Super Bowl—is not an easy task. It takes effort.

## THE MEANING OF TEAMWORK

On those occasions when I have taken over a poorly performing organization, one of the biggest problems I have found is that while everyone talked about teamwork, few people knew what it meant. They didn't know what a good team looked like, much less how to create one. Most organizations tell their people they want teamwork, and then let it go at that. They simply make the declaration and expect it to take shape on its own. They expect and hope that once the declaration is made, people will "work together." But what does "work together" mean anyway? Does it mean to agree on everything? Does it mean to share resources? Does it mean to avoid conflict? Most organizations fail to even define what teamwork looks like, so it is no wonder that employees are confused.

Another obstacle to teamwork is that most organizations have internal processes and policies that actually drive people to work *apart*, not together. Let me give you just a few examples.

Most employee performance appraisals are done on an individual basis, and not the team to which he or she is part. However, how can you expect an individual to put the team first when he is critiqued only on his own individual performance?

The same thing applies to individual departments. For example, Quality has its goals. Manufacturing has its goals. Marketing has its goals. They are very seldom, if ever, in alignment with each other. How can you expect Marketing to work as a team with Quality when they don't have the same goals? In most organizations, one department doesn't even know what the other department's goals are! And they don't care. Why? Because they aren't compensated to know, or evaluated to care. They are compensated and evaluated only to care about their own goals.

I once ran a division in a large, so-called "matrix" organization. While each division was responsible for profit and loss, we all shared common manufacturing, marketing, and quality organizations. Manufacturing was supposed to support my division. But they were also supposed to support all the other divisions. Here was the inherent conflict: with limited resources, how would they choose which division to support?

As a member of the so-called executive "team" in this company,

I used to sit through marathon "beatings" (sorry, meant to say "meetings") where the president would demand better performance, and all his executives would throw blame at the other guys. All anyone wanted to do was get out of the room alive. Some team, huh?

This practice is commonplace in many organizations. They talk about teams, but they align all the organization policies against them.

## WHAT DO TEAMS LOOK LIKE?

In order to create a team-oriented company, you have to have a clear model as a guide. Sometimes it's easier to describe something by first agreeing on what it is not. Therefore, let's begin by clearing up some common misconceptions about teams.

### *Misconception #1: Teams are Free of Conflict*

Actually, it's quite the opposite. The best teams are not conflict-free. Without conflict, there can be no progress. Without conflict, teams can fall into "group-think," which prevents them from coming up with new, creative possibilities. Conflict is the tool that great teams use to sharpen their perspectives, uncover flaws in their approaches, and create fresh, revolutionary thinking.

Every effective team has conflict. In a business world of limited resources and seemingly unlimited challenges, conflict is ever present. But most teams will pretend it doesn't exist, or just bury it from the boss's sight. They hope somehow it will just go away. People generally believe that conflict is not a good thing and that good teams don't have it, so they are afraid the boss will not be pleased if he or she finds it.

I once led a team that pretended not to have conflict. In group meetings, everyone "made nice." They would not raise issues and they would pretend conflict didn't exist. They would take potentially contentious issues "off-line," which meant the issues wouldn't get dealt with at all.

*Unresolved conflict never goes away on its own.*

Unresolved conflict often festers and causes negative feelings among teams. This is because they feel their opinions are not valued and their needs are not being met. So, the idea is not to ignore conflict; rather, the idea is to uncover it and teach teams how to manage it.

Knowing that conflict existed but was not being addressed where it needed to be – at the senior leadership level – I had to force it out. I would raise the contentious issues and wouldn't let anybody out of the room until they were addressed. But more importantly, as the leader I always let them know that conflict was okay and that I expected them to address it, not bury it.

### *Misconception #2: Teams always agree with Each Other*

The worst thing that a leader can have are team members always agreeing with each other. If your team members think you expect them to agree, you will lose two of the most powerful attributes of a superstar team: originality and creative thought.

You want some of your team members to be "outliers," in that they bring offbeat thinking to the group. After all, some of the greatest advances, if not all the greatest advances in the world have resulted from outlier thinking. The key thing to remember is that when first introduced, an outlier is always a bad idea. Perhaps it really *is* a bad idea, but you can't know that until it is thoroughly examined.

Be sure your teams know that it is okay to disagree and that, in fact, you expect disagreement. This is very important because if you don't tell them, most teams won't know it. They should strive for extraordinary results, not agreement for agreement's sake.

### *Misconception #3: Team Members like Each Other*

Let's face the facts, not everyone likes everyone else in this world. The same is true in the workplace. If people happen to like each other on a team, great. However, this is not necessary. What is necessary is that they *respect* each other.

I have had many effective teams where the members didn't like each other at all. However, because they respected each other and were highly committed to the mission, they produced spectacular results. I have been part of teams where I really disliked one of the other members, but respected their views and their ideas nonetheless.

Always remember that *like* is not an essential ingredient in successful teams; *results* are.

Now, let's examine the other side.

## WHAT IS A SUPERSTAR TEAM?

There are many definitions of a team. Here is my own:

*A team is a highly integrated, highly autonomous group of talented people who are highly committed to both the team and each other in the pursuit of extraordinary results.*

Let's look at each part of the definition.

"Highly integrated" means everyone on the team knows what everyone else is doing and is willing and anxious to help them. Unlike dysfunctional organizations where people work in a vacuum, not knowing or even caring what someone else is doing, in a high-performing company, one hand always knows what the other is doing.

The success of one of my teams perfectly illustrates this concept.

My team and I had just arrived in St. Louis for our industry's biggest trade show. We were excited to be there because we were ready to announce several new products that were sure to get the industry's attention. In fact, the future of our division rested on a successful launch at the show.

When we got there, half of our products were stuck in transit and not likely to arrive on time. So what did I do? Actually, nothing—I didn't need to. The team huddled and doled out assignments to each other according to the talents and abilities of each member. For example, one had the assignment of tracking down the products; another had the assignment of getting duplicate products from the home office; another had the assignment of re-configuring our trade show booth; and another was tasked with creating "virtual" representations that could be used if needed.

These guys were highly integrated, highly autonomous, and highly committed. While this may be a simple example, it illustrates how this team flawlessly executed everything from product development to product delivery. Each member knew who would complete a certain task most efficiently, and then they executed against that.

At Miller Ingenuity, our factory teams see the orders every day. They make their own manufacturing plans based upon when the orders are due. They decide what orders have to be produced today, and if so, they produce and ship them—all without a boss telling them what to do. If they learn a customer has an urgent need for a rush order, they move heaven and earth to make it happen.

## CREATING A SUPERSTAR TEAM ENVIRONMENT

A team-based framework doesn't just happen by itself. You need to take it in steps. Each step is as important as the others, beginning with the understanding that teams are *unnatural* in organizations. So, if you want teamwork in your organization, you have to create the framework for it—you can't simply ask for it and hope it happens.

You'd think that everyone would want to be part of a team. After all, many employees are deeply committed to their bowling teams. Don't all employees want to be part of a team? Well, actually no. Being part of a team is unnatural for employees, at least at the beginning. Most employees spend a lifetime in a work environment where they are individual contributors, not team players. One shouldn't underestimate the ingrained cultural bias against teams.

Being part of a team, accountable to the team, and accountable for a result that is beyond an individual's control can be inherently uncomfortable. Employees often ask themselves, "What happens if my teammate lets me down? What happens if the team can't reach its goal, but I can reach mine?"

Most employees naturally want to control their own destiny. To rely on someone else is uncomfortable. So, they are naturally skeptical about whether the whole team thing is a good idea.

Years ago, I developed a concept called "Team One" for my executive teams. While the concept is quite simple, it's actually very difficult, if not impossible, for some people to accept. "Team One" refers to the senior leadership team, whose job it is to run the overall company, not only a specific function, even though each of them has a responsibility for certain functions. As an example, my sales vice-president is expected to play on the senior leadership team. Yes, he runs the sales organization, but he also plays on my team. I expect him to put the senior leadership team's needs and objectives ahead of the sales team's needs.

This is especially difficult for a sales guy to accept. By nature, sales people are lone wolves. Thus, by the time a sales guy gets on the executive team, he has spent an entire career working on making the next deal. When you ask him to forego that next deal for the good of the executive team, he just goes ballistic.

I once had a sales guy on my executive team who couldn't accept this idea, and had a hard time even *understanding* the concept. He was bound by a career of devotion to short-term gains. To use a sports analogy, he was a professional golfer, not a member of a basketball team. I counseled him for months to get him to see the perspective and make the transition. He couldn't do it, so I asked him to leave. You know what, he was happy to leave, because the whole team thing was totally against his nature. He was a good guy, but the team thing was not for him.

When you introduce teams in your organization, the concept won't work for many of your employees; therefore, you'll have to help them understand, or, failing that, show them the door.

With the team framework in place, you need the right people. Never just fill a vacant position with someone who is qualified on paper only. Instead, make sure that you only hire superstars who fit into the culture of your company and its teams.

To make the best hiring choices, I have always used peer interviewing, even in the factory. Why? So your team can assess if the candidate would work well with them.

## THE SIX PRINCIPLES YOU NEED TO CREATE SUPERSTAR TEAMS

Broadly speaking, all the policies and resources of the organization must support the team concept. If any of these are not in alignment, they will impede the development and maintaining of teams. Thus, they must all be synergistically in support of each other.

1. **Make all organization goals support the one key metric—profit.**
   Perhaps the single most important thing you can do is to align your goals. Conflicting goals wreak havoc in organizations—they confuse the employees and create chaos, in addition to

destroying harmony and forcing people to compete against each other, rather than competing against the competition. They force people into a "me" and not "we" mindset.

Here is an example: The quality guys often have a goal of not letting anything out the back door, so they meet their goal of zero defects. On the other hand, the manufacturing guys want to shove everything out the back door no matter what the quality is, to meet their delivery goals. The sales guys want to meet their order goals without regard to the cost. Okay, maybe I am being a little facetious.

I have seen so many companies in which the individual functions met their goals, yet they still lost money! When Lehman Brothers went belly-up, many of the executives received big bonuses because they made their individual goals, and yet the company went bankrupt. How insane is that?

This is not to say that departments should not have their own goals. Rather, they must be aligned with the only thing that matters at the end of the day: profit.

2. **Align the incentive structure to support Goal One.**
This is really a very simple step. If the company hits the budgeted profit number, everyone gets an incentive; on the other hand, if it doesn't, no one does, and it doesn't matter how well a department performs. Though some will not like this because it forces interdependence, that is exactly what you want; that is, people who will put overall profit before departmental need.

This is a very powerful tool. Once a company I ran was in danger of not making the profit number. It was coming down to the last few weeks of the year. I was walking through the factory and one of the employees stopped me. He was very aware of "goal one" because we updated all employees monthly on our performance against the budget, which is essential for this plan to work. He told me he knew it was going to be close and asked me if there was anything else he could do to hit the profit budget! Imagine that, a factory employee worried about the company making its profit budget. Now, that is powerful!

3. **Incorporate the team into your hiring practices.**
Once you have the team concept in place, the worst thing you can do is to let anyone in the door that doesn't fit the profile of a good team player. Therefore, you need to query candidates on their views toward teams, rather than simply asking them if they are a team player. What would you expect them to say? Ask them related questions that might give you a clue.

Here is a list I like to use:

- In places you've worked in the past, how was the workload decided?
- If there was an issue in your department, how was it resolved?
- What was the best work environment in your career and why?
- What was the worst work environment in your career and why?
- When you think about the people you have worked with, were they generally helpful or not?
- What do you think is the best way to organize a department?
- In other places you worked, who had the best ideas?
- In other places you worked, how were conflicts resolved?
- How would you describe your ideal workplace?

Listen very carefully to the answers. They will give you clues as to whether or not this person is a team player. Don't offer any information about your company first, lest you give them clues to the "right" answers.

The last essential factor concerns peer interviewing. Don't ever let anyone get on the team unless they pass muster with the teammates with whom they will work, as they know best if the chemistry is right and whether the candidate would fit in.

**4. Teach team conflict resolution techniques.**
Effective teams will always have to resolve conflicts. Although this is a good thing if channeled properly, you don't just throw them into the conflict pool and hope they can swim; instead, give them the tools they need. Here is a short list.

- Start by teaching them that conflict is not to be avoided. In fact, they should seek to uncover conflict and use it for the good of the team.
- Rule one in conflict resolution is to have respect for the other team members. Respect for them as people and respect for their ideas.
- Train all members on how to facilitate discussions designed to bring out and deal with conflict. Also, teach them that conflict almost always has to be drawn out and won't appear magically. Some people have to be encouraged to make their opinions known, while others have to be toned down a bit because they want to dominate the discussion.
- Some conflicts can't be resolved by the team itself. Make sure they know and are comfortable with bringing a particularly sticky issue to a higher level in the organization.
- If, as the leader, you aren't well-versed in conflict resolution, get some expert help. A good industrial psychologist can help you with this.

## 5. Constantly nurture and protect the team.

Teams won't sustain themselves over time if they aren't constantly nurtured and reinforced. There are several ways to do this:

- Celebrate the team's achievements every chance you get. Do this publicly for all to see. I like to take out full-page ads in the local newspaper with pictures of the team and what it achieved. Everyone likes to see themselves in the paper and brag to their neighbors.
- Reward the team every chance you get. It doesn't have to be a lot of money (although it can be based upon the achievement), it can be something as simple as dinner out for the team and their spouses, or a pizza party thrown in their honor.
- Celebrate the team's *failures* every chance you get. This may sound weird but it is an integral part of team nurturing. They need to know that failure is okay. The whole organization needs to know that failure is okay, for without failure, there is no trying, and without trying, there is no success. Thus, let your teams fail without fear.
- Do a team check-up from time to time. For example, ask them how they're doing both individually and as a group. In addition, ask them what is working well and what is not, and how you can help them make the team even better than it is.
- Protect the team. To do this, sometimes you have to take a team member out. From time to time, you will find that a team member is no longer suitable to be part of it. Often, the team will tell you this themselves, so it is important to not let someone who has soured on the team idea infect the rest of the group. Ask them to leave the company. Once one of my executives tried to throw my executive assistant under the bus by blaming her for not scheduling a meeting he missed. I don't know if she scheduled it or not, and I don't care. Because he blamed

her when he should have supported her, I dismissed him. He was a valuable resource, but not as valuable as protecting my team.

## 6. Start by building your own team.

As the leader, you have to build your own team before you can expect anyone else to do it. Too many leaders "expect from below what they are not willing to do above." Don't make the mistake of expecting team behavior from below when there is backstabbing left and right in the higher echelons of the company. Always remember that people in the organization are watching you all the time, and that they will take their cues from the top, so make sure the top gives the right cues.

Start by introducing the "Team One" concept to your senior leadership team. Don't underestimate the cultural impact this will have. It will most likely be a huge shift in their mindset and require a re-tooling of how they have to be going forward. You will really need to sell the concept. You need to do this carefully and thoroughly.

Get some outside help to do a "Team One" check-up to see where the senior leaders stand on the concept and how receptive they are to it. This is not a one-hour exercise, so I advise going offsite for a few days and really examine where you are and what the impact will be. This is very likely one of the most important things you will ever do. Don't make it a "check the box" exercise.

Whenever I have done this, I've engaged an industrial psychologist to facilitate and guide us through the process. Buckle up, because this process is probably going to involve a couple of really ugly days. However, now is the time to understand and face the ugly truth, as you don't want to walk away from that offsite without complete alignment.

Remember, if you don't get this right with the senior leaders, you have no chance in implementing it in the rest of the organization.

Once your employees consider teamwork as a core value in the organization, it is time to unleash your teams to develop your company's Innovational Potential™. The next chapter will demonstrate how this has taken place in several organizations, all of which most of you should be familiar with.

CHAPTER 5

# CASE STUDIES IN METAMORPHOSIS

The case studies shared in this chapter are devoted to those companies who foresaw changes approaching their industry and chose to embrace them rather than deny them.

## CASE STUDY: ENCYCLOPEDIA BRITANNICA

Encyclopedia Britannica looked into the future and saw the digital world approaching. However, unlike Kodak (who must have seen it too), Encyclopedia Britannica chose to prepare for it rather than burying its head in the sand hoping everything would turn out alright.

In 2010, after 244 years, it went out of print. However, the company had already realized that it was going out of print whether it liked it or not. In response to the evolution of digital media, the company purposely chose to make the transition to the digital world.

This was a gutsy decision. This was a "bet the company" decision that only had two possible outcomes: to go out of business or not. You can be sure the transition to digital was hugely expensive and risky, and I can only imagine the angst its employees, leaders, board, and shareholders felt over it.

We can't know the trials and tribulations its CEO went through to convince all the stakeholders that this risky decision was necessary. The chances are they resisted and objected to it. Stakeholders tend to do this when their nice, comfortable world is threatened, as they don't want to confront an uncertain and radically different future; thus, they prefer their CEOs to tell them that everything is fine and will always be fine.

In psychological terms, this is called confirmation bias. We tend to surround ourselves with people and information that confirm what we already believe to be true, which is what most shareholders and CEOs do. As they want to believe the future will be as good as the past, they look for information that confirms their beliefs and reject anything that does not.

For Encyclopedia Britannica, the threats to its print business were everywhere. Wikipedia had a practically cost-free business model and the internet exists as a relatively free space for people seeking information. So why would anyone pay for an encyclopedia?

The threats to Encyclopedia Britannica were two-fold: the rise of free, up-to-the-minute digital information and the demise of print information. It had to find a way to address both, and it had to transform itself from a business with all print expertise to one that had all digital expertise. This was no small task. Imagine the transformation it had to make in the skill sets of its employees, and imagine the fear employees felt at leaving the only work-world they knew for one they didn't understand.

I have always said that transforming from a low-tech to a high-tech company is never about the technology, which is the easy part. Rather, the most difficult part of the transformation process always concerns people. In the case of Encyclopedia Britannica, the company not only had to change its technology skill set but it also had to abandon its door-to-door sales approach in place of a direct marketing one. Moreover, it had to change its editorial content creation time from weeks to minutes.

Just imagine the level of multi-tasking required during the transition. Radical business transformations commonly involve only a few large decisions, but also a million little ones. The million little ones during the transition are the most important. Encyclopedia Britannica's CEO had to be hands-on every step of the way, as should any CEO when undertaking the transition of a company.

Encyclopedia Britannica is still struggling to find its place in the digital world; thus, its transformation is not yet complete. Two lessons can be learned from this: first, the technology to move the company into the digital world was a simple process, and technology, as stated before, is always the easy part. In Britannica's case, the hardest part was its market transformation. Because it was late to the digital game, it had a hard time catching up. Arguably, it still hasn't. Since it came from the print world, digital markets and consumers have a hard time accepting it. Let's face it, when you think about digital books, you think Kindle, not Britannica, and when you think about where to go for knowledge, you think Google or Wikipedia, not Britannica. This is the uphill market battle they face. The other lesson here is that radical transformation from low to high-tech is a long, arduous journey. It is a metamorphosis, not an overnight event.

Consider the options Britannica had when it embarked on its journey—it was dying and by now would have been bankrupt; hence, selling the company before then would not have been an option. Its print assets were also useless in a digital world, and its brand was a dinosaur. The problem is that I don't believe the CEO viewed the brand that way. Instead, I think he and the shareholders viewed the brand as powerful and valuable, which it undoubtedly was in the print world, but not so in a digital one. Strong brands in one context or market do not necessarily translate into other markets or times.

For example, a strong brand in the 1950s was Studebaker, which was an upmarket car manufacturer. Despite being a strong brand, it would be foolish to think Studebaker would be an asset in 2018 just because it used to be in the 1950s. You couldn't dress up a Studebaker today and leverage the brand in today's market—it just wouldn't work because Studebaker is viewed as a car from the days of yore.

To further illustrate, do you remember Rock'em Sock'em Robots®? Not many do, but it was a very popular child's game in the '60s and a strong brand to boot. The game is so archaic that it would be near-impossible to launch it in today's world so successfully. The look and feel of the brand and the toy are very low-tech, and frankly, kind of clunky. It wouldn't be a strong brand in today's context and time, and to believe so would be a mistake. That is the mistake Britannica made—its brand was strong for the times in a print world, but not in today's digital world. Today, the Britannica brand is viewed as yesterday's educational source.

One strategic decision that the company could have made was to cut operating expenses to the bone and harvest the business, as this is often a better choice than to merely plow tons of transformation money into a business that can't be saved. In my view, Britannica made the wrong choice; it should have harvested. Before you choose to transform from a rust-belt organization to one that incorporates high-technology, it is important to conduct a very thorough "harvest-and-hold vs. growth-and-go" analysis. In its simplest form, this analysis estimates the cost of the growth-and-go transformation vs. the profit of harvest-and-hold. The major complicating factor lies in the assumptions made on both sides of the equation. What will it cost to complete the transformation? Whatever your assumptions are, you should double them. In my experience, transformation costs are always seriously underestimated, as well as assumptions regarding harvesting. Most CEOs assume they can harvest longer than they really can. Consequently, any assumptions you make on how long you can harvest should be cut in half. That will give you the most realistic forecast.

The only variable this analysis cannot account for is risk. During the harvest or growth period, both good and bad things will happen (mostly bad) that may not have been accounted for. So, you must discount your numbers with some reasonable assumptions to account for that. Without knowing your industry, I cannot tell you what to use here. If you are in an industry that is dying quickly (read: rust-belt), you need to account for a higher risk number than if you are in an industry that is slowly dying.

If you choose to harvest-and-hold, eliminate all unnecessary expenses; in doing this, you won't need salespeople, just an order taker or two, who could also combine their roles with that of customer service. Also, quality control would also be removed from the equation, and all marketing, advertising, and promotional expenses should also be cut. Further, there would be no need to go to any more trade shows. You won't need a human resource department. Outsource your hiring, if you need to hire at all. Outsource your accounting too. Cut absolutely everything that doesn't directly generate revenue.

Go all in if you decide to choose the growth-and-go plan. Don't be shy about providing the resource this effort needs to be successful, and what's more, don't implement the plan half-heartedly, or you'll end up starving it to death. It is important to promote the new brand and its products heavily. You need to be very aggressive about this because your competition will constantly try to depict you as "the rust-belt guys that couldn't possibly produce a high-technology product."

Now that we have examined a company transformation that is arguably failing, let's look at one example of an organization that succeeded, to see what lessons are there.

## CASE STUDY: NOKIA – FROM PAPER TO CELLPHONES

Nokia started as a paper mill in the late 1800s. It first morphed itself into a manufacturer of rubber tires and galoshes, then into military electronics, and eventually into cellphones. I cannot imagine a more dramatic rust-belt to high-technology transformation than that. In the 1990s, it sold its rubber and paper divisions to focus on cellphones. In fact, for 14 years, it sold more cellphones than any other company in the world. While it is still struggling in the smartphone market, its metamorphosis from boots to electronics is worth a lesson or two.

1. It had a grand and sweeping vision. Not a puny vision to be the best paper and boots company around. Instead, it chose an audacious vision. So should you. Why not imagine the most elegant, expansive, exciting future you can?

2. Nokia planned far out into the future. I have to believe it didn't stumble its way from a paper business to a worldwide cellphone manufacturer. You don't just take a couple of rubber engineers and tell them to start working on electronics. No, the expense, organizational resources and planning required had to be enormous. Your transformation plans need to be the same way. You shouldn't try to shove it all into one year or perhaps even into a decade. As the saying goes: "No wine before its time." Your mantra should be: "No transformation before its time."

3. In 1992, Nokia decided to go all in on emerging telecommunication markets. It divested itself of anything it didn't consider vital to them. This is a decision you will need to make in your transformation journey. At some point, you will have to divest yourself of the old to make room for expense and organization focus on the new. This will not only be a matter of finding the money for your transformation but also the focus. No organization—no matter how big—can focus on too many things at one time and be successful at all of them. You can't either, so don't try.

4. Be prepared to sell off your next-generation project if it doesn't continue to be successful. Nokia did this when it sold

its entire mobile division to Microsoft. Bear in mind that Nokia's next-generation idea used to be its mobile division. Like Nokia, you need to recognize when yesterday's winner becomes today's loser.

## CASE STUDY: CIRQUE DU SOLEIL®

This is one of my favorite case studies. Not only are there lessons here in reinvention but there are also lessons in how to fund an organization transformation by eliminating legacy expense.

In a nutshell, Cirque reinvented the circus—the dying industry that seemed to have no hope for the future. In fact, the premier circus, Barnum & Bailey, ended its 146-year run in 2017. I can't help but wonder why it didn't reinvent itself into a Cirque du Soleil? I know the answer to that. Barnum had its blinders on and mistakenly believed the circus would last forever. It believed it could trade on the strength of its brand forever. Maybe it would have if Cirque hadn't come along.

Cirque du Soleil® examined all the elements of a traditional circus to determine where the value was for the consumer, and more importantly, where it was not. It sounds simple, but then it eliminated the parts consumers really didn't care about and strengthened the parts consumers loved. Sounds a lot like jettisoning legacy products, doesn't it? Surprisingly, the parts consumers didn't care about were also the most expensive to maintain; in this case, elephants. In fact, it eliminated animals altogether, and nobody missed them! This is exactly what you should do: eliminate the parts of your product portfolio that are expensive to maintain and that your customers really don't care about and aren't willing to pay for if given a choice. That is how you fund your transformation.

In the English language, the words Cirque du Soleil mean "sun circus" or "circus of the sun." Now, the company could have called it that instead of using the term Cirque du Soleil.

However, that would have conveyed a tired old circus dressed up in new clothes. When you think about your transformation brand, think contemporary, think elegant, think avant-garde. Don't convey your new, transformed high-technology products while still dressed in old circus clothes.

Cirque du Soleil® invented a higher margin category of great entertainment because it attracts audiences with more disposable income than traditional circus goers; at the same time, it eliminated the most expensive parts of the traditional circus. The lesson here is when you consider what products and customers you want to target in your transformation, go for the least cost and highest disposable income in your markets.

Now that we have learned how a few other companies transformed themselves, it is time to ignite your own Innovational Potential™.

## CHAPTER 6

# IGNITING INNOVATIONAL POTENTIAL™: FROM RUST-BELT TO HIGH-TECH PRODUCTS

I am a business transformation expert. I take sleepy little rust-belt companies and turn them into global behemoths. In fact, I have never failed to triple the returns on everything I have touched. One thing I have learned in over 40 years of doing this is that every company – without exception – is a gold mine. All you have to do is find the hidden treasure that lies beneath.

This hidden treasure might be in the form of restructuring how you go to market. It might be in the form of creating what I call a Cirque du Soleil® culture—a team that is totally committed to performing on the edge of their abilities and sworn to do better tomorrow than they did today. Also, this culture could arise in the form of a never-ending blizzard of killer products. Products that destroy the competition and delight the customers; products that blaze new trails and return huge profits to the shareholders.

While this would be, indeed, fantastic, far too many companies are stuck in the wasteland of commodities—the dog-eat-dog world where everyone races to the bottom. Or they waste time and money on new products that never get out of the starting gate, and if they do, the returns are uncertain and paltry.

I can show you how any company can move from the underbelly of also-rans to the elite world of mega earnings. This can be done in a variety of ways. However, my favorite go-to method is to ignite a company's Innovational Potential™. This is a battle-tested method that has proven its astounding potential time and time again. To transform a company from Rust-Belt to High-Tech is a huge and complicated endeavor and carries massive risk if done incorrectly. However, it also carries an immense reward if done successfully. Just look at the margins Nokia made in paper compared to cell phones. In case you don't know, paper industry margins are around 6% compared to cellphone margins of around 68%.

## IGNITING A COMPANY'S INNOVATIONAL POTENTIAL™ IS A KEY ELEMENT OF TRANSFORMATION

To truly become a market leader and obtain superior profits, it is essential to disrupt the market. However, to disrupt the market, it is necessary to disrupt the company. Disrupting any company is very difficult. This is particularly true in rust-belt, old line, middle-market companies in so-called mature industries. The order of the day is disrupt or be disrupted. A perfect example of this axiom is what happened to Blockbuster. Netflix totally disrupted it. Now, who is gunning to disrupt Netflix? Amazon, the ultimate disrupter.

Disrupting the market requires "disruptional thinking." However, disruptional thinking is not a random act, and it's not a natural act either. It won't "just happen," as it needs to be forced. Disruptional thinking comes from repeatedly using a methodology that unleashes creativity—or, Innovational Potential. While every company has massive potential to innovate, most don't. Why is this? In my experience, it always boils down to one or more of four reasons.

1. *__Lack of belief:__* most people don't believe they are inherently

creative and therefore do not act accordingly. Hence, many companies don't believe they have the "right stuff" to innovate, and don't even try.

2. *Lack of methodology:* there is a methodology to ignite ideas and unleash creativity in any organization. However, many people believe creativity and innovation is a mystical beast that only appears in the minds of the Einsteins in the world.

3. *Lack of resources:* some companies try to employ creative methodologies but don't provide the resources for them to take root. They don't view "this creative stuff" as the real work and believe that if there is any time left over after "the real work" (there never is) then the creative stuff can begin.

4. *Lack of focus and commitment:* unleashing Innovational Potential takes laser-like focus and steely determination to see a project through, no matter what. Read the last sentence again. Are you prepared to dismiss good people if they can't or won't go along with the Innovational Potential program? Are you prepared to go toe-to-toe and nose-to-nose with your board if they want to shut it down? Trust me when I tell you, there will be plenty of naysayers all around, as starting down the Innovational Potential road is not for the faint at heart.

There are nine steps to igniting your company's Innovational Potential:

1) **As the CEO, you must put a stake in the ground that, no matter what, you are going to devote the time and resources to unlocking the company's Innovational Potential™.**
Gather the troops together and lay out your plan and vision. Make it bold and clear, and set high expectations for results regarding sales, margins, and timelines.

## 2) Tell people why this needs to be done.

Need a hint? Think of this word—survival—and it is a pretty safe assumption that most rust-belt companies are operating in survival mode. This is where you have to convince people that this whole, scary, weird thing is necessary. As this cannot be done in one company meeting or with a memo, I like to use a "drip" campaign, meaning that, over the course of a year or two, I use both economy and industry news to educate people on what is happening around them. In the rust-belt world, there has been no shortage of bad news, such as plant closings, layoffs, and relocations to China. What is less apparent, and what needs to be explained to your people, is how technology is destroying the rust-belt jobs that aren't being displaced by lower labor cost, or in other words— robots. Robots will be the disrupter of rust-belt jobs in the future. Between China and robots, it will be impossible to compete on the basis of cost. That is why you need to move into the high-technology world. Be very clear that this is not an optional program, so full participation is mandatory. You should explain that all job descriptions will be revised to include innovation responsibilities and a large part of future performance appraisals and compensation will be based upon it. This explanation will not only get their attention, but it will also scare them, which is why you talk about steps 4 and 5.

## 3) Hire a creativity consultant to conduct a company-wide survey to measure the current Innovational Potential™.

I once hired the ex-Chief Creativity Officer of the QVC home shopping network. That is weird, right? Why on earth would I hire an innovation guru from a shopping network? First, because under his leadership, QVC went from hundreds of millions to billions in sales. Second, because I wanted the most advanced and creative as far out-of-the-box of manufacturing as I could get. No incremental thinking—only revolutionary thinking. When you conduct your innovation survey, you might be surprised to learn your company is more creative than you think. In turn, your people may learn that they are more creative than they think they are. In fact, numerous studies have debunked the popular myth that all creative people are born that way; thus, creativity can be learned and taught at any age.

With survey results in hand, you now know what you need to go to work on. Feed the survey results back to employees. Tell them what needs to be done, meaning that *everyone* in the company will be trained in the principles and practices of creativity and innovation. This starts with basic brainstorming techniques and gets more sophisticated as time moves on. However, brainstorming is the starting point, as nobody can build upon an idea that has not been properly thought out. Brainstorming is what provides the raw material from which to build solid foundations. The idea is to generate new ideas all the time. At this point, leaders should expect 99% of all brainstorming ideas to go nowhere, while the remaining 1% should be fabulous.

**4) Provide the time for people to brainstorm and unlock their Innovational Potential.**
At Miller Ingenuity, we allow for and expect people to spend 20% of their time innovating. Because of this, we hire more people than we need for production so that they can achieve this. These days, our employees decide what problems or opportunities to brainstorm, and they decide where and when they will do it all, without a "boss" telling them what to work on.

**5) Provide the space and the environment to unlock Innovational Potential.**
I built an innovation space in the middle of the factory a number of years ago. Our employees named it "Creation Station." I call it a Google-like campus in the middle of a factory. It is a high-tech space designed and built to foster innovation, creativity, and collaboration. From the room

darkening windows to electronic whiteboards, to cushy lounge chairs and a ping-pong table, the room is wired for innovation. Our employees are not only allowed but encouraged to go into brainstorming mode in the Creation Station anytime they want. At any one time, on any day of the week, you will see our employees there just "working on stuff." But does the "stuff" they work on pay off? It does. From a million small improvements and ideas to lots of major ones, the payback came very quickly. However, it took a leap of faith to build the space. The Creation Station was a significant capital investment with a difficult to quantify return. You see, most CEOs won't bat an eyelash at spending $500K for a CNC machine. Why? Because they view it as an income-producing asset; likewise, so is my Creation Station. Here is a key difference between the two. The CNC machine has a finite useful life, and therefore, a finite production of income. In addition, it needs to be replaced; on the other hand, my Creation Station has an infinite and useful life of income production.

**6) Now comes the truly difficult part—asking for creativity sounds appealing to most, but really, it is not.**

There are several reasons why a leader may come up against a resistance to creativity.

- Some people who don't believe they can be creative never will be, no matter how much training you give them. Innovation is an all-hands exercise and those that can't contribute have to go.

77

- Many people, especially those in factories, have been trained to "check their brains at the door." For many people, this is a happy place. There's zero accountability, and all they have to think about is their bowling score. Most people like this can't or don't want to re-engage their minds—just try and convince them of the merits of participating in the program, but don't try too long. Remember, participation is mandatory and if anyone is allowed to be "not mandatory", it dilutes the whole effort. However, what if you can't convince them? The answer is simple: they have to go. Dismissing people that aren't participating will send a strong signal to the organization that you mean business. When the health and happiness people tell you that you can't terminate people who don't participate, kick them out of your office. Of course you can—as long as you set new expectations and give them reasonable time to comply.

7) **In the beginning of this sea-change, people will be afraid their ideas are no good, or that they don't have any ideas.**

Tell people you will give them lots of help in this area. As mentioned before, I hired the ex-Chief Creativity Officer from the QVC network to teach brainstorming to all employees and to ride shotgun with them for the better part of a year until they got the hang of it—and get the hang of it they did. At first, we gave them problems to solve, told them the time it should take to solve them and what tools they would need to do it. The process was very management structured, and within a year, employees picked the problems to solve, decided where and when to meet to solve them, gathered the tools and resources necessary, and then solved them—all without a boss telling them what to do.

8) **Prepare to bring in new talent that can support the newer products you'll end up making.**

High-tech products will be very different from your

traditional products, so it will take a different skill set than you currently have. Unless you have unlimited money (who does?) you'll probably need to swap out older legacy product employees for newer high-tech product employees. At the same time, you need to commit the employees you keep, by stating that, as legacy products phase out in favor of the high-tech products, they will be trained in the new products that are coming. Otherwise, legacy product employees will head for the door.

9) **Recognize, reward, and reinforce.**
This is the fun part! Every time my team comes up with a creative idea, I hire a professional photographer to take a group picture. Then, I put the picture in a full-page 4-color advertisement in the city newspaper congratulating and commending them for their achievement. You wouldn't believe the motivational power of this. People love to see themselves in the paper. They love to brag to their neighbors about being in the paper. Here is a bonus—it becomes a great recruiting tool when potential hires see how we recognize our employees.

Like my old Uncle Jim used to say, "If money isn't #1, I don't know what #2 is." You can talk intrinsic rewards until you're blue in the face, but without the money side, you're only giving people half the equation. I always give each member of the team a crisp $100 bill in front of the entire company.

Igniting your company's Innovational Potential™ is useless if you don't transform that potential into products, which is the subject of the next chapter.

CHAPTER 7

# FROM POTENTIAL TO PRODUCTS

Igniting the Innovational Potential™ of the company is a great beginning, but it is not the ultimate goal. The juices will be flowing, and your employees will be churning out one new product idea after another. However, they won't be generating high-technology product ideas, because they don't know how. They haven't lived in the high-technology world, and they don't know what they don't know.

The ideas they come up with will be useful in maintaining your legacy products. You don't want to turn that off or discourage it. Keep those ideas coming, so the innovation process becomes part of the company's DNA. It is important to take those churning ideas and turn them into high-technology products with high margins. That is the future you want to live in.

This is a complicated endeavor because the skill sets you probably have are at a rust-belt level of innovation. For decades, your employees have probably been doing the same things in the same way. One more little thing after another, one more incremental change after another—nothing radical or revolutionary. In fact, you may have a culture and operating policies that forbid anything radical or revolutionary. I would bet all your compensation, recognition and reward, and performance appraisals are all geared to and support "keep on keeping on."

Most rust-belt companies are very good at "not really new, but improved." You know what I mean. Brand extensions of your existing products. Small tweaks or slightly improved features. These improved features are probably asked for and specified by your customers. That's all well and good and will take you a little farther down the road, but it doesn't go very far in terms of margin or growth potential.

What you are aiming for are "new to the world" products; that is, products no one has seen before. These include products that satisfy a big unmet market need, clearly differentiates you from the competition, delights your customers, and that can be patented to protect you from competitors. Further, these are products your customers probably don't even know they need or want. It is most likely that your company probably isn't very good at this. In fact, rust-belt companies usually do not do this at all, or haven't tried to for many years.

***It's not a stereotype to say that most rust-belt companies are still living off innovations they made decades ago.***

This is part of the problem and the reason so many rust-belt companies don't leap to newer, higher technology products. They belabor under a false delusion that the innovations of decades ago will go on forever—they won't.

New-to-the-world products not only hold the most potential for the future, but they also hold the most profit in the future. However, the problem is that these types of products, whatever they may be, are completely foreign to your people. Your team has lived in the rust-belt world for decades, so this is what they are comfortable with, and they really don't want to do anything different—different is threatening and scary. When you attempt to develop new high-technology products, the chances are your team will have no idea what to develop, how to develop it, and how to commercialize it. It is a monumental task, and you are going to need a ton of help.

Transforming Innovational Potential™ to commercialized high-technology products is a three-part process:

**First:** *You have to find, select, and engage a contract product development firm that is really good at this.* (We'll cover that in detail in the next chapter.)

**Second:** *Line up their team and yours to produce and commercialize your first high-technology product.*

This is important because it gives your team a real-life high-technology product to work on as opposed to an academic exercise, such as if you simply hired a technology firm to teach your team how to do it. This is where your team begins to learn about the high-technology world and the high-technology development process.

Let me draw the comparisons between the rust-belt and high-technology development process. Rust-belt development cycles are usually a few weeks to a few months in length. Typically, these development ideas come from your customer. They ask you to solve a problem, and you do. More often than not, they even hand you a print to work from. Put simply, the process is thus: you cut a tool, make the part, ship it, and bill it all within a 6-month time frame, or even less, closer to 2-3 months. The risk is very low because you already have a buyer for it, there is practically no research and development, and the cost of the tool is low.

The problem with this is if the customer handed you a print, they own the part, not you. They can always give it to your competitor if you don't play nice and cut the price on demand. Also, the margins are consistent with the risk—very low. This is the world your team is used to. Predictable and comfortable. All within a relatively short lead time. There is a low risk of failure, and the cost of failure is low. It is a nice and comfortable place to live. I guarantee your stakeholders would prefer to stay here.

High-technology development cycles are very different. The customer doesn't ask you for it, and they might not even know they want it. The market for such a product may not yet exist and will need to be developed. The develop to ship-and-bill cycle, at least in the beginning, is years not months. When stakeholders are used to finite, predictable, and quick turns, they get dissatisfied in a hurry—especially boards. You'll be getting "where's the beef" questions constantly, and you'll have to continue to remind them that this "new stuff" isn't like the old. However, it is important not to simply draw comparisons that emphasize the expense and lead times. Every time you talk about the expense and lead times, also talk about the huge margins and new markets you'll obtain. Never talk only about the downside, but instead always talk about the upside in every conversation.

It is a "threat and opportunity" discussion. You need to constantly remind your board that there are threats out there. If you don't mitigate them, bad things will happen, and if you don't talk about this at every opportunity, they will be tempted to take the profits you are using to mitigate them in the form of dividends. Don't get me wrong; boards have the right—and in some cases, the obligation—to declare dividends. Just be sure they make informed decisions about this.

On the other hand, in the same discussion of "bad things happen if we don't..." you need to discuss all "the good things that will happen when we do..." Don't spend any more time on the dark side than is necessary. Otherwise, your stakeholders will get spooked and just shut down. On the other hand, if there is no dark side, your board won't give you the resources to avert it.

Remember, shareholders like dividends—not reinvestment—unless they are convinced reinvestment is absolutely necessary. It's your job to convince them it is. It is a constant sell job until you reach the point where the new high-technology products take hold and produce results.

Perhaps the most difficulty you will have is to keep these projects alive until they bear fruit. This is usually challenging, especially before you have a solid win. The longer it takes to get a solid win, the louder the drumbeat will be to kill the project. Don't underestimate the pressure you will feel from all sides to kill it. As long as the market feedback continues to be positive and the development is going according to plan, don't back off unless you are directed to by your board. What I have always told my board is this: "If at any time I conclude this is not a winner, you won't have to tell me to kill it. I'll kill it and tell you I did." And keep to that promise. Don't fall in love with your new product. Keep an open and objective mind toward it.

*Don't fall into the "sunk cost" trap. The sunk cost trap is where people believe so much money has been spent on a project that it doesn't make any sense to stop spending, no matter what.*

Blindly going forward is silly. If you come upon a time that the project doesn't make sense anymore, just kill it—and quickly. This can result from technology that was supposed to work but didn't. It can result either due to a market that was supposed to embrace it but didn't, or it can result from a combination of the two.

Let's assume in your heart you know that the new product is a winner. Let's assume all the signs of technology and market continue to be positive. Don't let your stakeholders pressure you into killing it. They will thank you later. One of my experiences with this came in a previous company I worked for. I introduced its first high-technology product, using the process I will outline later. I viewed the expenditure as an operating item that didn't require board approval. I didn't see any reason to review it with them until the product was far enough in development to actually have something to show them.

When I did present it to the board, half of them were against it.

They couldn't understand why I spent a significant amount of money on something so different that had never been done before. This reaction was completely understandable. As representatives of the shareholders, boards are supposed to question anything substantially out of the ordinary—this was perhaps the most out of the ordinary in the history of the company. It took nearly two years to develop the product fully, but it was a great success.

**Third:** *You need to create a learning organization through a backward integration of the product development firm's knowledge into your own team.*

While you need an outside organization to get the ball rolling, you don't want to be dependent on them in the future. As soon as is practical during the initial product development, you need to start a technology and knowledge transfer. If you picked the right product development partner, they will be very interested in helping you do this; on the other hand, if you picked the wrong partner, they will resist this process so they can continue to derive sales from you. However, you don't want to rush this technology/knowledge transfer because job #1 is to get the first new high-technology product out the door and start making money. If you move too quickly to move the whole thing inside, you'll stumble. I would say that, as a general rule, you would start this process formally after you are satisfied the first product is commercialized.

The timing of this is critical. You can't afford to do it until your new products are producing profit to pay for it. Waiting too long extends your dependency on them for much longer than necessary. After all, your contract product development firm may move on to other customers or go out of business, thus leaving you high and dry.

One thing you need to watch for before you start the transfer process is your employees. They may not be closely monitoring and controlling the development process, because the "outsiders are taking care of it." This can be very dangerous for two reasons. First, you should never let any outside organization be in complete and autonomous control. This results in nasty budget and commercial surprises. Second, your team will never learn this new high-technology stuff unless you press them to get deep into the details with your contract product development firm.

Now, let's get started with one of the most important decisions you will make—choosing an outside research and development team.

CHAPTER 8

# FROM PRODUCTS TO THE RIGHT PRODUCTS

When you enter the high-technology product development world, you will probably find it mysterious at first. It is truly uncharted territory because you have never done anything even close to it before. The landscape is fraught with minefields, unknowns, and complexity. It is easy to spend huge amounts of money on high-technology development and get absolutely nothing.

Consider this: if you are a rust-belt company, your product development process is completely different from what you need in the high-technology world. Everything you know about product development is wrong and outdated. All of your experience is useless. The most important decision you will face in the beginning will be how you will approach the brave new world of high-technology development. You basically have two options here.

1. Do you hire a team of designers and go it alone?
Or...
2. Do you engage a contract development firm?

This decision will determine whether you are successful in the new endeavor or a complete failure.

Let's look at both sides of this question. If you decide to hire your own team of designers, you will face several problems. Since you are a rust-belt company, you will find it difficult to recruit high-technology engineers. Why? Because high-technology engineers seek employers that offer them cool, sexy new products to develop. They want to work in a Silicon Valley-type company environment—rust-belt companies offer neither in the beginning. Another problem is your geographical rust-belt location will be a turn-off to them.

Thirty years ago, I was involved in recruiting high-tech engineers for a company I worked for, which was located in Cleveland, Ohio. I spent months in the Silicon Valley recruiting engineers. I threw a ton of money at candidates and a ton of other incentives. I never got to first base because no Silicon Valley engineer worth his salt would move to Cleveland. The reason was two-fold:

(1) 'Birds of a feather flock together', and they wouldn't find camaraderie and intellectual stimulation.
(2) High-technology engineers like the freedom of being able to walk a block down the street and get another job if they want to. Neither of these options was available in Cleveland, Ohio.

I learned the hard way that high-technology engineers are a very different kind of recruit. Money is not necessarily a motivator. In fact, the products we were trying to develop failed because senior leadership insisted on hiring engineers and wouldn't entertain engaging a contract development firm. Their view was that the company needed its own internal development capability and the only way to get that was by hiring.

That view is one I disagree with. I do agree that eventually, you need your own internal development capability, but that does not mean you have to start out that way. In fact, I would argue that you shouldn't. At a later point in the process, you will put a plan in place to transfer technology to the inside, but not in the beginning.

It is impossible to try to hire dozens of high-tech development engineers to develop your new high-tech products. Even if you could, at this point you would not want to add that much fixed expense. You simply cannot afford it at this point. Until you know that your new high-technology products will take hold, you need to keep expenses in the new endeavor to a minimum. Spend what you have to, but spend very wisely.

This means that you will need to find and select a contract development company that has the resources to match your requirements. While this is important, you also have to find an affordable company.

There are four strict rules in selecting a contract product development company. Moreover, these are inviolable. Miss any one of them and you will fail. I call them the four A's:

1) Affordable

2) Available

3) Action-oriented

4) Ability

Let us start with the *affordable* factor. You can spend an infinite amount of money on product development and get nothing from it. In fact, some studies have shown that nearly 95% of all new product developments fail. The chances are you will fall into the 95% unless you are very careful. The chances are you will fall into the 95% even if you are careful! In fact, when you discuss this with your board, be sure you set the expectation that you only have a 5% chance of being successful. The worst thing that can happen at the beginning of this journey is to spend all of your discretionary development dollars for nothing. If that happens, your whole strategy goes up in smoke. Also, your board is unlikely to give you any more money to try it again.

The best place to find an affordable company is in Asia. Many of them are quite competent and their cost is less than half of what a United States firm would charge. But just because a firm is affordable doesn't mean they meet the other criteria. Affordable is where you start, because if they don't meet that criterion, there is no reason to look at the other three. Also, it is important to check their references carefully to be sure they are not only affordable but also competent. I have found that most underdeveloped country firms are long on promises and short on delivery. They will promise you everything and then disappear.

The second requirement is that the firm you choose must be *available*. That means available on your terms and 24/7. If you want to do design reviews at 8 AM your time, it might be midnight for them—so be it. After all, you are the customer so you should not expect to have your team up at midnight—that is their obligation. If you pick the right partner, they will be very happy to do it.

Furthermore, when your team needs an impromptu answer in the middle of their night, a good partner will always have someone on standby to provide support and assistance. My go-to team answers email questions within the hour, no matter the time of day or night. You will need that kind of response because the deeper you get into a new high-technology development, especially when you are testing it on a customer, the questions and complications come fast and furious. This means the answers need to, as well.

Of course, their English language skills must be impeccable. This is not always the case with underdeveloped countries. Put them through an English language test like those that Upwork does with its contractors. However, just because they speak English does not mean they understand your culture, or your business lingo. You cannot assume "communication" is occurring just because they understand the words. Ask clarifying questions often. My Brazilian business partner is always checking this. He speaks excellent English. Nevertheless, whenever we have an important discussion, he will pause and say this: "Let me be sure I understand you *perfectly.*" Then, he will repeat back to me what he understood me to say. Often, we find we really did not understand each other perfectly and keep at it until we do. That is what you should often do with your product developer. Ask them often to tell you what they think you said, and also, keep at it until both of you are completely satisfied you are communicating, not just talking.

The third and perhaps most important requirement is they must be *action-oriented.* They must be committed to outcomes and results, not just research and development. They must move quickly when you need them to, and must be motivated to move heaven and earth to help you hit your goals and your deadlines. By the way, your goals should be a product you can sell, not just an elegant design.

You need to be very careful when evaluating whether a potential firm meets this requirement. Some cultures tend not to be as action-oriented as Americans. Generally speaking, product development firms tend to noodle on things—a lot. They do not like deadlines. They like to keep tweaking a product until there is nothing left to tweak, which, by the way, is never. Therefore, you need to be sure the team you pick is committed to getting the product out the back door. How do you know if that is their style? Ask them about the most recent development projects they worked on. Also, ask them what their objective was and how long it took them to get to it. If they answer in terms of a product that would be commercialized by a certain date—you have the right firm. On the other hand, if their answer is in terms of an Alpha, Beta, or prototype design, then you had better dig in a little deeper. It is possible their last client gave them the objective of an Alpha and that is all they paid for. If that is the case, you cannot blame the design firm for not being sales action-oriented. You want a design firm that is committed to getting you a product that produces sales in the shortest amount of time. You do not want a design firm that will hand you a design and wish you the best of luck. Unfortunately, that is what most of them do, so you have to be very careful here.

The fourth requirement is the easiest. They must have the *ability* to do what you want. You can assess this easily by looking at their past portfolio and checking with their previous customers. These days, high-tech product developers need all the skill sets to fulfill the ability requirement. That means you have to look for a firm that is well versed in hardware, software, firmware, mechanical and electronic design, communications, sensors, and packaging. Also, you should be careful in choosing a firm that has all the talent you need, not just some of it, as you do not want to 'sub out' parts of the development to another company. The more you have to do this, the more possibility of errors and missteps in the handoffs. Do not settle for a design firm that cannot do it all.

Finally, assuming you have picked a firm that meets your requirements, also known as the four A's, know that your work has just begun. Expectations and deliverables have to be very clear on both sides. That means clear, written specifications for product performance, which is usually a collaborative process between the two companies. At the beginning of a new development, specifications will be broad. When you first imagine a new product, you do not really know exactly what it needs to be, so it would be impossible to nail down the exact specifications.

Therefore, you should take this process one step at a time. Your initial specification may be limited to patent and technology research to see what is out there. The second step might be a specification and agreement for producing what is called a "minimum viable product", or MVP, with broad performance parameters that would be tightened up later. Do not try to develop the final product in the early stages, as that would only be impossible and frustrating for both sides. It would also be expensive because you would have to start, stop, and redo and revise previous work.

You will have to be comfortable with the idea of substantial ambiguity in the beginning. You will not know what the product will be, and you will not know what it will do, except in general terms. Further, it is almost guaranteed that you will not know what the features, functionality, and cost will be in the beginning. Just be sure and set up what I call "must have's" and "cannot's" in the beginning. Here is what I mean. As an example, set the expectation that the product "cannot exceed" a certain cost or that the product "must have" a certain functionality. What happens if it doesn't? You don't pay them. That would also be a red flag to stop and reassess where the development is going.

## UNDERSTANDING HOW A CONTRACT PRODUCT DEVELOPMENT FIRM WORKS

Now that you have engaged a product development firm, as the CEO, it is important that you understand how they work.

In the beginning, the product development firm will assign an account relationship manager. This person will be responsible for the overall project and the relationship with your company. He will decide the skills and resources to be assigned to your project. Even though he will act more like a business than a technical manager, he needs to be technically educated and experienced. Otherwise, he will not be able to make good skills assignment decisions. It is crucial that your team and the account relationship manager have an excellent relationship.

Once he is in place, he will assign as many engineers as necessary to get the job done, along with an overall technical project manager. In part, this decision is based upon how many engineers you are paying for. Technically speaking, you will not be paying per engineer. You will pay based upon engineering hours on a per hour basis. By the way, you should not need to pay any more than about $35 per engineering hour.

## STARTING AND STOPPING IS A BAD THING

Here is some bad news. You cannot manage this expense as one would usually do in marketing or advertising. Simply put, you can't turn it off and on at will. That is because if you turn it off, the relationship manager will send your engineers to other projects, and moreover, you would lose efficiency, knowledge, and inertia. This would be hard to recover from and would add further cost to the development.

Considering a high-technology development process usually takes two to three years, the business cycle may dictate your actions. If sales take a dive and your board is pressuring you to reduce expenses, you may not have any choice, or you may have to choose other operating expenses to cut to keep development in place. If you have to cut development expenses, talk it over with your relationship manager and be certain you are aware of the impact of any choice you make.

## ONE FINAL WORD

My old Uncle Jim once gave me some sage advice. He said, "People don't screw people they know and like. They only screw people they don't know, or know but don't like."

I do not know about you, but I try not to do business with people I do not like. However, that is not always possible, because now and then, you have a customer who acts like the backside of a horse. However, I do not choose that.

When you pick a product development firm, it is important that you like them as people. After all, you will spend countless and endless hours with them. The fate of your company and your career is largely in their hands. Also, your team is likely to be more successful if they are working with a firm they like and respect, which can make a huge difference.

The other important reason is for technology transfer purposes. A good contract development firm should be working toward the day you do not need them anymore. That day will never come unless they teach your team how to do what they do. Such teaching and learning can only occur in an atmosphere of like, respect, and trust.

Now that you have picked the right product development firm, it is time to get started developing your first high-tech product.

CHAPTER 9

# FROM VAPORWARE TO REALWARE

In the rust-belt world, product development is straightforward. It is hardly product development at all; rather, it is more like application development as you are simply applying what you know to brand extensions. What usually happens is this: Mr. Customer hands you a print. Then, you cut the tool, make the part, and ship the part. On the other hand, envision a situation where Mr. Customer expresses an interest in something you have not made before and asks you to develop it. All of this takes place in a short time frame, typically over 8-12 weeks. It involves no risk because Mr. Customer already told you he would buy it, and you can manufacture it using familiar materials and processes.

This is not the case with high-tech products. The risk is high, and you will be working with unknown and unfamiliar technologies, materials, and processes. Also, the cost of failure is very high. If you miss the mark on what the market wants or what the customer is willing to pay for, you will have spent a huge amount of development money only to scrap it and go back to the drawing board.

However, you say: "Before I start the development, I will talk to my customers, so I know exactly what they want." Do not rely on that. Most customers have no idea what they really want in a "never-seen-before product." Henry Ford was rumored to say, "If

I'd asked people what they wanted, they would have said faster horses." So be sure you do not spend a lot of money on a faster horse.

So it goes with your customers. Oh sure, if they are only asking for tweaks to an existing product or a replacement product for a better price, they will quite specifically tell you what they want. However, when you are dealing in "new to the world" products, this is hardly the case. They have no idea what they want until they see it; therefore, you have to find the cheapest way to give them a look at it before you spend a ton of money. More elegantly stated, you need what is called: a *Minimum Viable Product* (MVP). There are plenty of books on the subject of MVPs so I will not go into detail about the process here. I just want to talk to you about the business and practical side of it from a CEO's perspective.

Let's begin by covering a few executive-level conditions and absolutes you must set in front of your design team before they even start. The MVP must be the following and no more. I say "no more" because the idea behind an MVP is to make it inexpensively and get it out there fast:

- Margins must be at least 70%.

- The product must offer multiple features needed by customers that the competition does not provide.

- Strong and multiple patents must protect the product.

- Electronic components must be off-the-shelf. This is primarily how you achieve high margins.

- Minimum product features and inexpensive off-the-shelf packaging and hardware will be used for round one of the MVP. This way, you are not wasting time and money on tooling you would otherwise throw away later.

Okay, so you have set the conditions for the MVP. Let us look at how the process might unfold from a practical point of view. Pretend for a moment that your team has come up with an idea for an automatic potato peeler. They have done some preliminary market research, and amazingly, no one has invented one yet. Your team has talked to a few potential customers and reaffirmed what they already know—that peeling a potato is a nuisance and it is just dying for a solution.

Your team sets out to develop an MVP for the soon-to-be-famous "AutoPeel." What kind of electronics should it have? What should the hardware look like? Should it be in the shape of a ball that wraps around the potato? Should it be shaped to be held in one's hand? Should it attach to a can opener for dual use? Should it have a LED light on it for use in lower light conditions as you might find in a kitchen at night?

You cannot know the answer to any of those questions until you get what is called a user experience. So what does a MVP'er do? He takes his best guess at the minimum features and buys the cheapest off-the-shelf hardware and packaging he can find just to get it out in the field for customer feedback based on user experience.

Let me give you a real-world example. I once put an extremely sophisticated electronic device in an off-the-shelf yellow traffic cone just to be able to position the electronics somewhere and get it out for user feedback. Was the ultimate plan to package it in a traffic cone? Of course not. That's just an object to hold the "brains" of the product. When we first took it to the field, we explained to the customer the traffic cone was just a placeholder. This road test gave us the chance to ask specific questions about packaging. What size would you want it to be? What is the maximum weight it can be?

Aside from packaging, what features does AutoPeel need to have? Should it on run off a mobile device or should it run with an onboard switch? What about software? What kind does it need and what does it need to do? What about communications and sensors? Does it need to communicate with other internet-of-things devices in the kitchen? If so, does it need to be on a ZigBee or another communication protocol?

You can see that, even for something as simple as an automated potato peeler, you can spend endless amounts of money and be dead wrong when it gets to the field; therefore, it is best practice not to do it this way. Think in terms of what MVP stands for—the minimum viable product—which means the bare minimum in form, fit, and function to get it into the field for user feedback. The feedback is so much more relevant when the customer can actually see, hear, and touch something, than an abstract conversation about what they want in an automatic potato peeler. They do not know what they want in an automatic potato peeler. They do not even think they need an automatic potato peeler until they see one.

Do not gather user feedback from a handful of customers. *Get as large a sampling as you can.* In consumer markets, this could be in the thousands. In industrial markets, it would certainly be dozens or more. The point is, do not let anyone, or only a handful of customers, dictate your design choices. Moreover, try to find the commonality among all of them. What you do not want to do is to design fifty-seven flavors of your new product to satisfy everyone.

Beware that the sales team will want the engineers to develop fifty-seven flavors so that every customer is satisfied and they have more tools in the sales box. The engineers will want to do the same thing so they can lay birth to the most beautiful new product baby ever conceived. Both teams are happy as clams to spend your money to no end. Stop them both in their tracks.

Of course, you will move to a "new and improved" design once you have 'sold the hell out of' AutoPeel V.1. However, not until then. You might go to V.1 to stay ahead of the competition or because of technology advances. An example of this is why broadband companies are constantly making their pipes bigger and faster. Now bear in mind that they may not want to. After all, their pipes work just fine. Moreover, it is expensive to make them bigger and faster. However, the gaming industry forces them to. In the case of the potato peeler, it might need an internet connection for health monitoring, performance reporting, or unbelievably, potato peeler gaming playoffs! You get the point. You may not want to make a potato peeler ultra, but technology may force you to. If you do, make sure you bake in lots of margin. Remember a cardinal rule in the world of high-technology products: *The customer only gets those additional features he is willing to pay for.*

The information detailed above is round one of MVP. Now comes a critical time where you have to decide if you should invest in bonus rounds. This is important because the bonus rounds get more expensive. So far, you have only spent a little money and you are not deeply committed to the project.

*Listen very carefully to what the customers tell you.*
*Listen carefully to what the design team tells you.*
*They both want the same thing—everything.*

You have to ask yourself and the team some hard questions. What did you really learn in the field? Were the customers excited over what they saw or were they only mildly interested? Did you get any strong "I'd buy it if it could do this" signals? If you received tepid reactions all the way around, seriously consider killing it.

Let me give you a real-life example. Miller Ingenuity developed a suite of safety products that prevent railroad workers from being killed. It senses the approach of a train and warns the track workers in time to get out of the way. It was a first of its kind and has been very successful in the market. It is called ZoneGuard™.

When we demonstrated the ZoneGuard™ round one MVP to our first customer, I was sweating bullets. Sure, we had done lab simulations and thousands of tests on a track behind our plant. However, this was the first time we had taken the product out to a real live railroad in front of real live customers. The stakes were high. The customer was a major player in the rail industry. The CEO and his four division general managers were all at the test site. We were all silently awaiting the approach of the train to see if ZoneGuard™ would alert us to its approach—it performed flawlessly.

At that point, the CEO started clapping and cheering! When is the last time you saw a customer do that over one of your product demos? Then, he put his arm around me and congratulated me for developing it. Later on, he made this statement: "We have the technology to send a man to the moon, but we can't stop track workers from getting killed—until ZoneGuard." That was when I knew I had a winner. Therefore, I went to MVP round two.

If I had not received such positive and enthusiastic praise, I might not have gone to round two of the MVP. Instead, I probably would have gathered more user feedback before making a decision. There is no clear-cut line about whether you should go to round two or not. If all feedback is positive and enthusiastic, it is an easy decision, whereas if all feedback is negative or non-committal, the answer is also easy. The chances are you will have a variety of mixed reactions, which is why the decision can be so difficult.

This is why you need to be in the field for every one of these demonstrations to get the unfiltered feedback directly from the customer. I say unfiltered because your team is likely to put a happy face on the field trials. After all, they are the ones who recommended the AutoPeel in the first place, and they are the ones that are pushing you to keep funding it. The engineers will want you to know they did everything right, even if they did not. The sales team will want you to think they are doing a good job of selling it, even if they are not. I am not saying they are lying to you. I am just saying it is natural for people very close to the product to hear and see what they want to hear and see. That is why you need to be there to hear and see for yourself.

In its simplest explanation, you take the common feedback and do revision number two of your MVP AutoPeel. In a very simple product, you may only need one revision. However, in the types of products you will be interested in, you will need more like three to four hardware revisions and at least four to six software and firmware revisions. If the product is still viable after those revisions, it is time to stop tweaking and move on the path toward production and commercialization. The point is do not tweak it to death for the sake of tweaking it and making it more elegant. Build in only what it needs and only what customers are willing to pay for. At some point, you need to commercialize it and save future features for future releases of the product. Your model should be the iPhone. Apple did not wait to release the iPhone until it was at Version 7. As Apple has added features over the years, it has released new models that have increased overall sales. Do not wait until you have all the features anyone could possibly want to commercialize it. You will run out of money by then. More importantly, it will give your competitors time to release their own AutoPeel.

Revisions of the MVP are a process of discovery. Your team should be helping the customer discover what he can do with the product. Your engineers are discovering what they can do with the product to satisfy the customer's needs. Let me use another iPhone example. I will bet with every new iPhone or Android device you have ever had, you only knew about half of what it could do. Then, you set out on a process of discovery to learn about the other half, some of which you will be interested in and some of which you will not. Unlike the iPhone, where you are famously on your own in the discovery process, in your MVP, you want to lead the customer by the hand. You need to do that so you do not include features the customer does not want, or more importantly, will not pay for. Be careful in this phase, and be especially aware of the "shiny new object" effect. A new whizz-bang toy can conjure up a million features the customer may potentially want. However, the customer will not pay for a million whiz-bang features—they will expect you to pay for them. That is why it is crucial to nail down what they really need, and what they will be prepared to pay for.

You should plan for adding features, but that should come later. Get them hooked on the product first and start making sales before you go hog wild into the land of "feature creep." There will be plenty of time and profit later to introduce new and improved versions.

*Listen carefully at every stage of the MVP and keep a record of what they are asking for so you can incorporate them later. However, don't even think about incorporating everything a customer wants—ever.*

If most of the customers want a certain feature in the future, you should design it in and add it to new and improved models; on the other hand, if only a few customers want a certain feature in the future, forget it. You can't support a million variants even if some of your customers are willing to pay for it. Configuration management would be a nightmare.

At every revision, your design choices get narrower, especially in hardware. As design choices narrow, they get more expensive. Your first major decision will be in production hardware and packaging so make it a good one. If you make the wrong one, it is very expensive and time consuming to turn the clock back. Once you've finally decided on the hardware footprint, you are very limited in what you can shove into it such as sensors, communications devices, and the like. Lead times on cutting the tools and producing the hardware parts can be expensive and long, so you really need to be certain before you take that step.

Software is a little more pliable but it is expensive to develop.

Firmware is easily changed over the internet; for example, if Mr. Customer wants the AutoPeel to send automated reports and health monitoring to him, this can be implemented quickly and relatively inexpensively with firmware. Some customers will want health monitoring and some will not. Just be sure you charge handsomely for any customized features. The real money in high-tech products is in data, not the device itself. Many customers will pay you to collect the raw data and give it to them in a usable meaningful fashion. Margins in this can be as high as 90%, so you will want to develop that side of the business.

## A FINAL WORD

Always remember that the MVP is a business process, not a design one. Although it has major elements of design, equally important is the business case to be made every step of the way. It is your job to incorporate hard-nosed profit-and-loss decisions into the mix. It would be a mistake to allow it to be a design adventure for your engineers and a free ride for your customers. Keep in mind engineers like to play and customers like to spend your money. Don't let them.

Along your journey, you will encounter critical inflection points. Missing them can mean the difference between success and failure, which is the subject of the next chapter.

CHAPTER 10

# REFLECTING ON INFLECTIONS

During your metamorphosis, you will reach several inflection points. These are important because not only can they signal significant progress, but also significant danger. Some inflection points will be very clear and unmistakable. Some will be very subtle, so you have to watch for them closely. Some will signal good news and reaffirm your decisions. In some cases, positive inflection points may be your cue to accelerate your plan. Some will be bad news and a signal you need to make a course correction, so you must be alert to them, and when they occur, be ready to take decisive and swift action.

These inflection points will occur in one or more of the following three areas:

a) The market

b) The competition

c) People

Let's look at each one of them in turn.

## MARKET INFLECTION POINTS

When you start your metamorphosis, the market won't even

notice or react to it. When you first introduce your first new high-technology product, the market will not take it seriously. What you will find from the market is indifference. You should not expect any "aha" or "wow" moments. After all, up to this point, your company is only known for rust-belt products. When the market responds with indifference, you should not take that as a sign that the new product is no good and you are going down the wrong path. You need to give it time to permeate. This will most likely be a long process.

The market will begin to react slowly as you implement your disruptive positioning and marketing plans. However, once your disruptive marketing programs take hold, one of two things will happen: either the market starts noticing and reacting favorably, or it doesn't.

Favorable market reactions will include requests for quotes or demonstrations of the new product, lots of "hits" on your digital assets—your website and social media—which promote the product, and feedback from the field through your sales team. These are all more subtle, so you have to watch for them closely. When I introduce a new high-technology product, I review all market reactions at least weekly, which I highly recommend.

You should see these signs within a year of introducing the product and launching your disruptive marketing program. If you do not, it is time to understand why not. The "why not" will either be because the product is a bust and not needed or wanted by the market, or because your disruptive marketing program is ineffective. What you need to understand clearly at this point is which one it is.

Knowing which one it is can be difficult, especially if the new product breaks new ground in a market that has not yet developed for it. If the market has to be developed, you need to be patient and continue developing it with disruptive marketing. In these cases, the market has to be educated and informed as to why the new product is beneficial and worthy of the market's attention.

*The clearest way you can determine if the product is a bust is through direct customer feedback. When they see it in action, they will either yawn, tear it apart because it doesn't work properly, or get excited about it. That will tell you everything you need to know.*

## COMPETITOR INFLECTION POINTS

Early on, your competitors in the high-technology space won't even notice you, and if they do, they won't take you seriously; rather, they will simply ignore you. The longer they behave this way, the better it is for you. Once they do take notice and take you seriously, they will begin to react. Their reactions will be an inflection point that you are on the right path. However, be aware that they will react severely and aggressively. I know I would if a new competitor appeared.

When I become aware of a new competitor threat, I always choose to put a bullet in them before they can get entrenched. It is easier and cheaper to dispose of a new entrant earlier than later. Once they are entrenched, it becomes much more difficult and expensive to deal with them. Once your competitors view you as a threat, you can expect them to do one of the following:

• Threaten you with a patent infringement suit. Most patent infringement threats are meritless. The threatening competitor is simply attempting to stop you in your tracks. You should consult your patent attorney before you do anything.

• Start a marketing campaign designed to discredit your company and your products. If it were me, I would pound on the point that a rust-belt company is not qualified to develop a high-technology product.

- If a competitor thinks your product is better than theirs, they may attempt to buy the rights to it, or even attempt an outright acquisition of your company. This might not necessarily be a bad thing, depending upon what they are offering. Consider such offers very carefully.

- Some might just ignore you and hope you go away. These competitors would have assumed you won't go the distance and don't pose a threat. Of course, that is ideal and what you should hope for, but certainly don't count on it.

- Demands that you stop using your brand mark because it infringes on theirs. This could be a competitor in your industry, or it could be a company outside of your industry. If you did a careful job of researching your mark, this should not be a problem, especially if the demand comes from a company with a similar mark outside of your industry. Consult with your trademark attorney.

- Finally, a competitor may start acting like you. They may even start making the same product claims as you—even if they never did prior. They may modify their product to perform more like yours if they think yours is better. This is good and bad news. The good news would be you are on the right track regarding features and performance. The bad news is you may have shown them how they can compete against you more effectively.

## PEOPLE INFLECTION POINTS

At the beginning of your metamorphosis, no one will take you seriously. After all, the metamorphosis plan is so audacious and unlike anything the company has done before, so who can blame them? For quite a while, after it gets started, they won't take it seriously. Therefore, it doesn't threaten anyone.

At some point, usually about the time you are rolling out your

MVP, maybe a little before, it will dawn on them that this is a serious endeavor. That is when some of the villagers will come up the hill to kill Frankenstein.

You see, some of your employees have been waiting and hoping for this nonsense to die off. They want it to die off because either they don't believe in it to begin with, they are fearful of the change, or they feel they are inadequate and won't measure up to the new standards high-technology products will create. These employees will be a threat to your efforts. You will recognize who they are. They are the ones that sit on the sidelines asking disqualifying, naysaying questions about the process and the new products. They always jump to the "why it can't be done" instead of "how it can be done." They constantly throw roadblocks in the way. They are negative in product development meetings and are the ones that operate by stealth. What's more, they will never come out against it openly; however, they will be sniping from the woods and you might not even know it.

Sometimes they give you clear signs that they are not on board. Once I was with one of my sales guys meeting with a major customer. The question of our new high-technology product came up. My sales guy told the customer we were "out of our element" with the high-technology product. Now, why on earth would he say something that stupid, even if he believed it? The answer is simple: because he wanted to scuttle the effort, that is why. Guess what happened to him?

I wrote about these types of employees in my first book, *Burnarounds: Unlocking the Double Digit Profit Code.* I called them "the enemy within." The enemy within hates anything new. The enemy within drags his butt into work but can't wait to get to the bowling alley. The enemy within seeks comfort at all cost. Anything that disturbs that comfort is a threat and must, therefore, be eliminated.

Once the enemies within realize this is not going away, they will work to stop it in its tracks. If these enemies are in positions of authority and power (which often they are), they can wreak havoc on your metamorphosis in ways you won't even know about. They could even destroy it. Thus, you have to find them and invite them to work for another company.

Do this quickly once you are sure who they are. Give them one chance to get on board, and if they don't, terminate them. Not only will this eliminate a threat but it will send a message to other employees.

The metamorphosis will generate plenty of anxiety and fear. Even I have felt anxiety and doubt from time to time. It is perfectly natural for fair-minded employees to have these doubts. As I wrote before, provide the comfort, training, coaching, and support they need to get on the right side, and if they don't, it is time for them to leave.

## INFLECTION POINTS WON'T BE CONSISTENT

In a perfect world, all the inflection point stars would align. You would see either all positive or all negative inflection points, which would make for easy decision making. Sorry to break the bad news to you but that is not the way it happens.

*Inflection points are a lot like the economy. Some economic indicators point to expansion, some to contraction. Usually, the economic indicators are a mixed bag of good and not so good. Hard to make sense out of that.*

Your inflection points will behave the same way. Customer feedback might be good, but not great. The product may perform flawlessly for a while in field testing and then some software bugs might show up, or your competitors might not even notice you at all. Also, you might only receive a small order and not the significant one you were hoping for, or you might get a huge order and nothing more for six months. All of these scenarios have happened to me. Inflection points present you with nuanced decisions. It is crucial that you watch them closely.

In this chapter, we touched on people inflection points. However, people are the most critical part of your metamorphosis and not technology—which we'll cover in the next chapter.

CHAPTER 11

# TECHNOLOGY IS EASY— PEOPLE ARE HARD

Killer technologies are easy to come by. It seems like almost every day a new technology is launched. It is never about technology. When a company matches technology to a market need that is dying to be disrupted—voila! Super success. Not so fast.

Technology is the easy part. People are the hard part. So many companies spend so much money, so much time, and so much attention on technology that they ignore the people side of the equation. This is a big mistake.

## THERE ARE NO COOL KIDS

By now you should be well on your way to developing cool, new, high-technology products. You've been through your MVP, made some tweaks or maybe major changes with your "spend-and-see" program, and you're pretty sure you have a winner. Here's the bad news. That was the easy part. Now you have to develop your organization to manage the dichotomy between the rust-belt and high-tech worlds. Now starts the tough stuff.

It is critically important that you maintain the profit stream from your legacy products while you are bringing the high-tech products online. This will take a minimum of two years to achieve, possibly even longer. In addition to the product development cycle, you may have to develop the market too. Depending on the new products, the market may not yet be ready for them. You may be in a position of what is known as a "first mover" strategy. First movers have to plow new ground and develop a market for their products. Think of it as iPhone 1, before anybody even knew what an iPhone was or why they would even want one. Apple had to create a yearning and need in the market for such devices where none existed before. This process is expensive and time-consuming. The outcome is uncertain. You won't know if the market takes to your cool new product until it does or until it doesn't.

At this point, you will have hired high-tech people to work on the high-tech products. If you're not careful, the "old guard" will start thinking of them as the "cool kids." Remember the cool kids in high school? Didn't you just hate them? Didn't you want to see them pulled down from their perches?

The same dynamic will take place in your organization. You have to be very clear that the "old guard" is just as important as the newbie techies. Otherwise, the old guard will try and pull them down. Or they might just leave the company, leaving critical legacy product gaps behind.

So how do you do this? As with most things, it starts with the 3 C's of super communications:

❖ Clear
❖ Convincing
❖ Compelling

*Early on and often, call an all-employee meeting and reinforce your belief that there are no "cool kids," and the legacy people are just as important as the high-tech people.* In fact, every time there is a win in the high-tech or legacy products business, celebrate it and communicate it. The chances are you will have to look hard in the legacy products to find wins because those products are stable, "Steady Eddies" without a lot going on to talk about. Nevertheless, dig hard and find them.

## MAKE A COMMITMENT TO TRAIN AND BEGIN

If your legacy people think they'll be out of a job after the high-tech world takes center stage, they won't hang around long enough to see that happen. That would put your "bread and butter" business in jeopardy.

Commit that nobody will be out of a job when the legacy products start to disappear. Naturally, you have to condition that promise on their willingness and ability to be trained in the high-tech products. As an example, you probably aren't going to make a punch press operator into a degreed engineer. However, you could show him the path to an electronic technician. Or you could train him on installing the new products in the field. That is just one example of how you can transition existing skill sets into the new world. By the way, the legacy people won't believe you will do this until you do—so do it fast. When they make good progress in the training programs, recognize and reward them.

You should also find ways and projects a little out of the mainstream to excite the legacy employees. Doing the mundane, boring old things while the cool kids get all the cool toys can grow old pretty fast. Have them work on their own new product developments, even if you don't expect a return. Better yet, let them decide what new products they want to develop, then give them some time and resources to work on them.

You may be in a situation where legacy products are going down faster than high-tech products are coming up. Try to avoid the temptation to lay off legacy products people. Remember the promise you made? Now, I know in this situation that a lack of market demand is what can cause a legacy products layoff. However, people won't believe that is what caused it. They will believe you broke your promise and that the high-tech products were the culprit. If the legacy products are going down faster than you thought they would, you may end up with more payroll than you would like until you can place the legacy people into high-tech positions. You must be willing to do this or people will start to bail on you. The first time you don't honor the commitment you made to keep everyone, no one will believe anything else you say—ever.

Further, you will find some people are unwilling or unable to make the transition from legacy to high-tech. After all, changing what you do for a living can be scary. Some people don't want to have to think as hard as they will have to in a high-tech job compared to the rust-belt world. When you find this, give them plenty of outplacement support in finding another job and a fair severance package to help them bridge the financial gap until they do.

## LEADING THE MULTI-CULTURAL TEAM

In the beginning, the team (i.e., your contract product developer and your internal people) will almost exclusively comprise engineering people. As the process unfolds, you'll bring in sales, marketing, and production groups. As the development proceeds, the tasks the team takes on become more complicated—and critical.

The multi-functional nature of the team dictates that the leader must be very high up in your organization. However, the high risk, high cost and high potential for failure of the efforts dictates that the CEO must lead it. This is not something you can check in on every once in a while to see how it is going; you need to be actively and constantly involved.

Trust me when I tell you that even the most well-intentioned teams will go off the rails if they aren't closely controlled. The engineers will want to develop a perfect product; the manufacturing team will want to develop a product that is cheap and easy to make, and salespeople will want to develop a product that has everything the customer could ever want or hope for. Accordingly, neither option is practical or affordable.

The way to avoid negative outcomes is through maintaining tight control and constant communication. Bringing the team together often is critical.

I would say more often is better than less often. Don't have the meetings so far apart the team is compelled to communicate via email. You would be surprised what gets lost or misinterpreted in an email. Depending on the complexity of the project, my advice would be no less than once a week, and more often for more complex projects.

As the CEO, you have to lead and be engaged in every meeting. I know what you are saying, "I hate detail, and it is up to my people to be in the weeds, not me." I would normally agree with you but not in this case. This is the place where you have to do a deep dive into the details. You have to understand the technology, its place in the market, and where this project is going up close and personal. Remember when I said you'll make a few major decisions and a million minor ones that count? This is the place where you'll make most of them. You would be amazed at how far and fast this process can drift off if you don't maintain control.

Practically speaking, us CEOs do have other things we need to do and other places we need to be. Fair enough. Whenever I can't make the meeting personally or by phone, I have it recorded and listen to it later. I don't give my proxy to anyone, and I carefully review the actions taken, planned, and the decisions made in the meeting.

At this point in your metamorphosis, you will already have carefully planned, designed, and produced a killer product that no one knows about or takes seriously. It is time to change that with disruptional positioning, which is the subject of the next chapter.

CHAPTER 12

# DISRUPTIONAL POSITIONING

Now it is time to decide what your positioning will be in the market. What market space will you own? How will you position yourself against your competitors? What will your positioning be in the minds of your customers?

Picking the proper positioning is a crucial process. If you stake out a position against Goliath, you'll run out of money before you can make a dent in him. And understand this—really understand this: it won't matter if you have a product that is far superior to Goliath's. If you go head to head with him, you will lose so don't do it. But what if your team developed a product that really is superior to Goliath's? You have two choices. Sell the rights to it to Goliath, or position yourself to go around him, under him, or over him. The point is this is the part where creativity in positioning determines if you win or lose, particularly against big, strong, and well-funded competitors.

Positioning is a strategic decision. Positioning should be your grandest vision of where the company could be in the market if it had new high-technology products. This is not the time to put a square peg in a square hole just because it fits. Now is the time to make new holes.

Start by discovering what I call the "positioning sweet spot."

This is the place where the following conditions are present:

- A large unmet customer need that *is not already protected* by competitor patents.

- A position in the market where you can win.

- Hot industry issues that have not already been claimed by another brand.

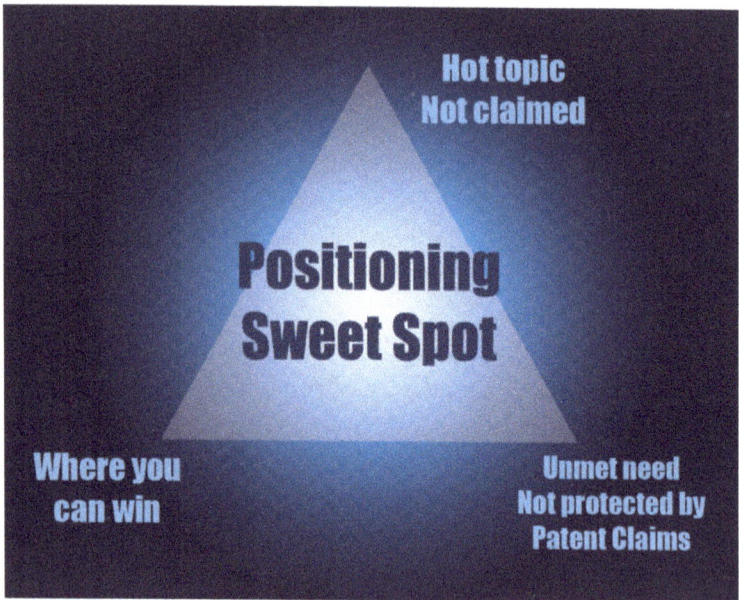

Meeting a large unmet customer need is fairly standard in marketing 101, but this is where most companies stop looking. Don't stop there. Keep digging.

Analyze every potential competitor's patent claims anywhere even close to the unmet need you are trying to solve. Weaknesses in these patent claims give you clues as to the real unmet need.

Let's use the famous AutoPeel example again. Anyone can see an unmet need in the market for an automatic potato peeler.

Everyone hates the time and hassle it takes to peel potatoes. Let's assume a few companies have developed an auto peeling product. Examine their patent claims to see what they reveal about unmet needs.

Put all the competitors on an Excel spreadsheet side by side, and examine every claim. See where commonality exists. Maybe the patent claims that it wholly addresses all of the features and benefits customers want, but that is unlikely. What is more likely is that the patent claims address a combination of three things:

1. **Prior art doesn't exist.**
   If you are not familiar with patent law (if not, it is highly recommended you become familiar with it), prior art would be evidence that your potato peeler invention already exists. Of course, if that is the case, a patent would not be awarded. This is where most development engineers start. They try and design the product around any prior art claims. That does not necessarily produce the best product, although it does produce a product that can potentially be patented. What you are looking for here are weaknesses in their patent claims, which I will elaborate upon later.

2. **Their own design capabilities.**
   As an example, a company with a primarily mechanical design expertise will focus their patent claims on mechanical design ideas. Thus, the patent claims also give you clues as to the competitor's design capabilities.

3. **The features they think the market wants.**
   Bear in mind; the competitors are probably making educated (or maybe not educated) guesses at this point, because up until the patent filing, they haven't produced a minimum viable product, so they can't know what the market wants. Speaking of minimum viable product, the chances are your competitors won't take that approach, which puts you at an advantage right from the start. It is quite probable that

your competitors don't know what the market wants. A close examination of the patent claims in relation to what the market really wants can sometimes reveal some gaping holes – holes you can exploit.

Let's take a look at an imaginary one to use as an example. The AutoPeel competitor device only senses the position of the potato with one sensing device, so they built patent claims around that. You should ask the following questions:

- Why did they design the product with only one sensing device?

- Was it because of prior art?

- Was it because they couldn't figure out how to design multiple sensors, or perhaps they designed only one in to keep cost down?

These are all good questions. Some you will find answers to, others you can only speculate. But think deeply about the answers. Probe and probe and probe. Don't stop until you have really dug deep.

Why not design more than one sensor into the peeler? Would more than one make the product more reliable, more robust, and more attractive? Would more than one make it more user-friendly? You can't know the answers to these questions until you get the minimum viable product in the field and collect user feedback. However, weaknesses in competitor patent claims give you a good place to start.

Now you have unearthed some unmet needs through the use of weaknesses in patent claims. Now you can move on to the second criteria: It has to be an unmet need *where you can actually win.*

After all, you can have a cool, new, patented product that the market loves and still get clobbered by the competition. But, for the sake of argument, let's assume an imaginary company, Ace Space Travel, has developed a product around the unmet demand for consumer space travel. Despite having a killer product the competition does not have and which might fill such a demand perfectly, Ace Space Travel has no credibility in the space market. No matter how good its product is, it could never win there because there are too many big guys with too many deep pockets ready to pounce on them. While none of them "own" space travel yet as a brand, one of them will. It just will not be Ace Space Travel. Always remember, just because an unmet need exists, that does not mean you can win there. Unmet needs are a good place to start but do not end there. Look for the third criteria before deciding.

The third criteria, which I find particularly fascinating, regards hot industry issues that have not already been claimed by another brand. Pinpointing hot industry issues is a simple task—simply ask yourself what the hot-button issues are in your industry. What is the number one thing that everyone always talks about as being "the most important?" In the healthcare industry, it is patient safety. In the airline industry, it might be fuel prices. In fast food, it might be how long it takes someone to get through the drive-through.

On the other hand, finding hot industry issues that haven't already been claimed by another brand is tough. For example, think about LifeLock, PC Matic, or MyPillow. Those companies already own those spaces in the minds of consumers. If you are going to own a market space from a brand point of view, you have to be the first company the market thinks of. In fact, you have to be the only company the market thinks of.

You can't claim a hot issue after the world already knows about it. It is best if you can claim the issue before the market fully realizes it. But how do you do that? By drinking Tito's vodka.

Tito's is a perfect example of branding a hot issue before anyone else. Years ago, Tito's claimed its vodka was gluten-free. It built its whole brand around that claim. Bear in mind, this was long before gluten intolerance was in fashion like it is today. Now, restaurants and food manufacturers are scrambling to produce gluten-free products. In the case of Tito's, they own that space in the vodka industry. Although most vodkas are gluten-free, it is too late for them to claim that space. Tito's already owns it. In their case, the company recognized that gluten-free products would soon be all the rage.

In my own company, Miller Ingenuity owns the safety space in the rail industry. Its tagline is Safety Starts Here, which conveys what Miller is all about—safety. When it comes to safety, Miller has your back.

**You need to think broadly and expansively about how to promote your brand. Don't just run trade publication ads.**

But Miller didn't stop with a tagline—it moved into the safety seminar space. I joined the board of The Safe America Foundation, a worldwide organization that promotes safety in all areas and across all industries. These efforts put Miller on the global stage and solidly positioned it as a global safety leader.

It is conceivable that a competitor might come along and try to claim itself as the "safety brand" in the industry; however, this would be difficult and costly since Miller has already claimed that space. A situation like this could be compared to the Acme Identity Theft Company trying to push aside LifeLock. When consumers think identity theft, they will not think Acme. LifeLock already owns that positioning. It would be extremely expensive and nearly impossible for Acme to unseat them.

This is what you need to do with your new brand: stake out a position that is big, expansive, and not already claimed by a competitor. Be sure it meets a large unmet need and where you can win. Don't go head-to-head with a competitor for the same small space—go around them and over them; go bigger than them; and moreover, go more outrageous than them. Produce one, or a few, great ideas that are astonishing and unpredictable. In short, hit them in a place they don't expect and can't recover from.

Make your vision grand and sweeping. Don't think small—small is boring and will not achieve much. Small won't inspire your people to go anywhere but the bowling alley. Don't think like Acme. Your vision should be to transform your company, as well as the market and industry. You can always narrow your vision later if you have to. But don't start with a narrow vision. Don't start with a narrow product focus.

Remember the Nokia case study. It started with paper and arguably redefined the cellphone industry (for a while, at least until the iPhone came along.) That is the kind of sweeping vision you should have. Do you think Nokia knew every step it had to take and every move it had to make decades in advance? Hardly.

You've heard this before—you don't have to know how to get there; you just have to start. It sounds corny, but I believe it is true that the universe provides once you set your intention. In light of this, set your intention and then just start. You don't need a grand plan; in fact, the so-called strategic plans of most companies are useless anyway.

However, note that if your vision is truly grand and sweeping, it will be the hardest thing you will ever achieve in your entire career. If it is not, then you picked a puny vision. Know that you'll want to give up many times. When you know in your heart of hearts, it is time to give up—don't! When this happens, it is a sure sign it is time to keep going and push harder.

Let's get a little more specific on positioning. What is McDonald's positioning in the marketplace? What are the features of a

McDonald's double cheeseburger? How is that different than anybody else's double cheeseburger? Is it the special sauce? I don't think they even put that on the double cheeseburger. Also, does McDonald's tout the features of its double cheeseburger in its brand promise? Would you drive further to a McDonald's for a double cheeseburger than to a Culver's?

Nobody can sell a hamburger based on features alone—they all look the same. The hamburger landscape is what I call "featureless." Everything blends in, and one is unrecognizable from another.

That is the world you live in with rust-belt products. Another way to say featureless is "commodities." You can't differentiate one hamburger from another. You cannot differentiate one rust-belt product from another. You should not even try.

So how does McDonald's position itself in the featureless world of double cheeseburgers? It doesn't. It doesn't even try.

McDonald's positioning is this: fast and furious (okay, without the furious part). You know when you go to a McDonald's you'll get in and out of the drive-through fast. McDonald's knows this and spends an extraordinary amount of time and money to deliver on that brand promise. It designs its menus with speed of cooking in mind. It measures the amount of time it takes to get through a drive-through and sets objectives to improve. It designs its parking lots and adds automated drive-throughs to support its positioning.

McDonald's doesn't waste time trying to make a better double cheeseburger. No one would know it if they did, and what's more, no one would care, because their customers typically care about one thing and one thing only—speed. That is the key benefit.

When developing your positioning, focus on the one or two key benefits most important to your customer. Don't waste time or money developing a better tasting cheeseburger when what your customers care about most is getting anything they can shove into their mouths fast.

Now that you have staked out your positioning, it is time to unleash a flurry of creative and disruptive branding, which is the subject of the next chapter.

CHAPTER 13

# DISRUPTIONAL BRANDING

I don't know about you, but I love this part of the process. This is the part where you get to see the fruit of your labors. I love it when I disrupt a market, take my competitors by surprise, and delight my customers. In one sense, this is the final output of all the product development work you have been doing. On the other hand, if you don't do this part right, you will have wasted a ton of product development money. If you do not do this part right, you will have built a better mousetrap, but no one will know about it, and no one will buy it.

*Disruptional branding has to start years before you are ready to unleash your cool, new, high-technology product.*

Why? Because you need to prepare the market for the "new you" long before the "new you" unveils new products. If all you have ever introduced to the market has been rust-belt products, and if you do not re-brand the company well in advance, the market will not believe you are capable of high-technology products. In a sense, this phase is convincing the market to believe something that is not yet necessarily true—that you are something more than a rust-belt company; you are a high-technology company.

So you need to rebrand the company. That takes time and

foresight. You start by imagining the kind of products you will be developing and branding the company around them.

Think broadly about the future you imagine for the company. You do not want to lock your company or your branding into any one "thing" or product. Going back to the AutoPeel example, the company brand shouldn't be "the AutoPeeler guys." Thinking broadly again, if the entry into the kitchen appliance market was AutoPeel, it would not want to limit itself to that one product. Instead, it should think more broadly and see itself as entering the kitchen appliance market, and that AutoPeel is only their entry product. They could further develop the brand by calling it "Kitchen Convenience at Your Fingertips" or maybe even "Done for You: Fast Kitchen Gadgets" or "Look Ma, No Hands Appliances." How about this one: "A sexier new you because you are in the gym while the gadgets are doing your kitchen work."

The rust-belt market is not quick to embrace rebranding. In fact, rust-belt markets are not quick to embrace anything. These markets move at a snail's pace and do not like change. Therefore, you have to give it time to take hold, and you have to spend money on it. A decent rebranding effort will cost $100K if it costs a dime, but spend it strategically and wisely. Don't just start placing trade publication ads—be creative and contemporary. More on that in the next chapter.

You should look into the future and imagine what you want and need the brand to be in five years' time. Then, pick a believable and credible middle ground to change it to first, perhaps a year or two out. However, have your plan in place for where the brand needs to go in its endgame.

Do not try and change your brand without professional help. It is an expensive endeavor and needs to be done correctly. You need an expert to help you with this to make sure you get it right.

Almost before the ink is dry on your rebranding 101, you should be planning your rebranding 102. But how do you decide what rebranding 102 should be?

## WHAT YOUR BRAND SHOULD AND SHOULD NOT BE

### *I. Boring is the enemy of breaking through.*

The number one objective of any branding message is to *break through*. It is not to convey a message. It is not to sell a product. It is not to distinguish your company in the market. Those are all secondary objectives. Whatever your number two or three objectives are, they are meaningless if you do not break through.

Your brand should never be boring! The market hates boring. Boring gets lost in the noise of a world already suffering from digital overload. Customers are not going to be interested in your story unless it is distinctive. They have enough in their lives and work worlds that, unless your branding messaging is quite extraordinary, it does not matter to them. Even if it is extraordinary, they might not care. This is what you are up against.

Believe it or not, the rust-belt market hates boring too. It just doesn't know it because it is used to the "same old, same old." The rust-belt market has been anesthetized with trade publication ads that don't convey anything and aren't seen by anybody. You can shine in a rust-belt market with just a little bit of creativity.

The most successful brands are anything but boring. Witness the LifeLock commercials featuring a bank robbery. Now that is not boring! If LifeLock ran a spot featuring a guy in a suit explaining why you should go with LifeLock how interesting would that be? How impactful would that be? And how about that LifeLock dentist commercial? Bear in mind that LifeLock is involved in one of the most serious high-

technology-based industries in the world—cybercrime—
and yet they chose to make light of it with its branding and
commercials.

## II. *Successful brands are memorable and comforting.*

People seek comfort and reassurance in their lives. Give this
to them with your brand. Where does "in good hands" come
from? You guessed it—Allstate. It is memorable, and you
can identify with the comfort of being "in good hands."

See if you can finish these brand taglines: "For the best
night's sleep in the whole wide world…." If you guessed
MyPillow, you are correct. It went a step further by singing
the tagline using nostalgic '60s type music. Why did they
use '60s type music? It targets their primary market of Baby
Boomers, so it makes perfect sense to use Baby Boomer
comfort music. It makes sense to subtly remind them how
long it has been since they really had a good night's sleep.

There are great branding lessons to learn from MyPillow,
which include:

- It knows exactly who its target market is, and its entire
  message and branding are developed around it. Also,
  notice that it doesn't target Millennials. You don't see
  them in its commercials, only 50- to 60-year-olds.
- Its branding is memorable, snappy, and comforting. It
  takes baby boomers back to a time of better, happier,
  care-free days. It wants them to remember the times
  when they slept like logs and yearn for those times
  again. It is a perfect set-up of creating awareness and
  need for the pillow.
- It focuses on the benefit of the pillow—sleeping. Only
  near the end of its commercials does it talk about
  features.
- It uses nostalgic, comforting, happy-go-lucky music as

opposed to just using a script and testimonials.

• Finally, it is not a confusing brand. You can tell exactly what MyPillow is just by reading the name of the product and the brand message. Let me give you just one example of brand confusion. Ever see the commercial for BDO? I am not quite sure what BDO is, but I think they are a "we consult on everything" variant of the remnants of the "big six" accounting firms. After seeing their brand dozens of times, all I know is their tagline, which is "people who know, know BDO." Obviously, I am not one of those "people who know" because I still have no idea what their brand stands for. Don't make that mistake with your brand— make it very clear and "idiot proof."

Let's try another tagline quiz: "A less than a one-inch incision leads to..." Kudos to you if you guessed—The Laser Spine Institute—and Kudos to them for planting that brand in your mind. In fact, if you Google the words "less than a one inch incision," the results will take you right to the Laser Spine Institute website. That is a beautiful brand tagline. It conveys the feature of the small incision with the benefit of the procedure – all in one sentence. That is not easy to do. Besides, did you catch how memorable and comforting that brand is? No big hole in your back. The procedure is over quickly. A lifetime of standing tall. Now that is comforting.

Do you suppose The Laser Spine Institute is the only company out there making small incisions in the back? If you Google "minimally invasive spine surgery" you come up with nearly a million hits. Minimally invasive surgery is done all the time. However, The Laser Spine Institute was the first one to claim that space with creative comfort branding. If a competitor tried to claim it now, they would always be known as "the other guys," not the experts.

*Branding can position you as "the expert" and "the only expert," even if you are not. Further, branding can help you claim that space before anyone else does. That is the awesome power of creative branding.*

Here is a great example of a comfort brand—AAG, the reverse mortgage company. Its brand features Tom Selleck as the pitchman. Good old comfortable Tom. People are comforted when they watch him. After all, he used to play a private eye in the '80s. Now he plays the New York City Police commissioner on the television show *The Blue Bloods*. I can tell you that there is nothing more comforting than good old Tom telling you everything is going to be fine if you just get a reverse mortgage.

When you imagine what your brand should be, think comfort food. I know that sounds silly, but try it. Conjure up images of mashed potatoes, meatloaf, or a big bowl of hot chicken noodle soup. What is it about comfort food that actually comforts you? Is it the actual food or the memories it brings forth? Is it the taste of the food, or is it the optimism you feel about the future when you eat it? Or the great memories of the past. Either way, it puts you in a good mood, and people are more likely to buy when they are in a good mood than when they are in a bad one.

That is what your brand should be—comfort food for your customers. A brand that conjures up good times of the past or hope for the future. This is what your brand should deliver . . . which leads us to the third principle of a terrific brand.

### III. *Effective brands appeal to emotion, not logic.*

Have you ever seen a Johnson & Johnson baby powder commercial? What is the essence of the Johnson & Johnson baby powder brand? It is not chemicals. It is not that it will keep your baby dry. It is not that it will keep your baby smelling good. It is none of those things, for those are all features, and none of them is a benefit.

Johnson & Johnson's brand promise is that if you use the product, your baby will be happy, healthy, and smiling all the time. On top of this, they further assure that because of the baby powder you used, he or she will go to an Ivy League school and live a happy life. Okay, I am a little facetious here...but not much.

The other half of the brand promise is you will feel good about yourself and be optimistic for the future of your baby. That is a lot to get from talcum powder, but that is their brand promise. You just never examined it from an analytic point of view.

You've heard it said that people decide on emotions, then use logic to justify the decision. You can buy a generic baby powder a lot cheaper than Johnson & Johnson, but you won't because of the emotion tied up in the brand. However, notice that Johnson & Johnson also gives you all the scientific reasons why its product is superior. Aha! Just what you needed to hear! You know that generic is just as good, but you have already decided to buy Johnson & Johnson based on your emotions. However, now the company has wisely handed you logic to back up the decision you already made on emotion.

Let's look at another emotion-based brand. Only this one missed the mark by just one word! "A Place for Mom" provides assisted living, memory care, and nursing home services. The national spokesman is Joan Lunden. Using her, its brand message is full of emotion about how you should be taking care of dear old mom. The best way to do that is by sticking her in *A Place for Mom*. Okay, so they used emotions and then they back it up with logic and facts. But did you notice they aren't talking about dear old dad?

What happened to him? Aren't dads allowed in *A Place for Mom*? Well statistically, dads don't live as long as moms, but that is not the reason they use mom. Mom conjures up more emotion than dad. Sorry, dad.

The only catch is that they wrecked it with one word, and it's not excluding dad. The word is "place." To me, that conjures up sticking mom into a "place," like a book on a shelf, or a thing to be put somewhere and forgotten. I would have used "home." Having mom in a "home" feels better than having her in a place. Now, I appreciate that opinions can vary on this. Using the term "home" could elicit negative feelings of a "rest home," where mom is stuck and forgotten. Still, I feel that "home" is more of a comfort food for the brand than "place," if you will.

Your brand needs to be the same way. *Everyone* buys on emotion. Not so in your industry, you say?

I know what you are saying. "That emotion stuff might work with your mother, but it won't work in the hardcore, gravel-and-guts products I sell." Maybe. Let's see. I don't think it gets much more gravel and guts than a potato peeler. Would you agree?

How would emotion work with our soon-to-be-famous "AutoPeel?" Let's use that as an example. What emotional buttons could you push with your brand message? How about more time to spend with the kids because you are not manually peeling a dozen potatoes for an hour? Or what about making Mom feel guilty because she isn't, and how AutoPeel can take that guilt away? How about more time with your favorite television program while AutoPeel is doing all the work? Or how about how you'll feel sexier because AutoPeel will be working, while you are working out? Trust me, if you can elicit emotion from a potato peeler, you can use emotion for any other product. Just be sure to start with the emotional benefit, not the product benefit. The product benefit comes second when logic wants something to justify the purchase.

Test your brand promise with as many people as you can before you cast it in stone. A good and inexpensive way to do that is by using a website called Pickfu.com, which provides polling and opinion services between multi-variants quickly and inexpensively through the use of paid survey panels. I often use it to test one book title against another and one brand promise against another. You can pick the number of people you want to survey, along with the educational level you want to pay for. I seldom feel the need for surveying more than 200 people and the results always come back in less than two days.

IV. *Effective brand promises link attributes while disclosing detriments.*

I love this one because it multiplies your branding and marketing dollars tenfold. There are tons of products out there that have unintended consequences, or detriments to their use. Hence, If you can link an attribute of yours that neutralizes or improves on the detriment of one of these brands, you'll get the benefit of their weaknesses and marketing dollars.

Take this example. Everyone knows that taking statins to lower cholesterol lowers CoQ-10 levels. That is a bad thing, right? I don't know. I don't even know if I buy the "everyone knows" part. All I know is a CoQ-10 manufacturer convinced me that is what statins do. So now that I am convinced that statins lower CoQ-10, I need to boost my CoQ-10 by buying their product. They did all this without once specifying how much lower my CoQ-10 levels would be after statin use, or even what my CoQ-10 levels should be with or without statins. Nice! Anyway, since it linked statins to CoQ-10, it gets the benefit of all the branding and advertising dollars the big pharma statin companies do. Let's see how we could use this with the famous AutoPeel.

Everybody knows that handling poultry spreads salmonella, so why on earth would you want to cut the chicken and then peel the potato? Sure, you might wash your hands between the two activities, but you might not wash off all the salmonella bacteria. You can see how this would work. In your branding and advertising, you link the two together, so it is clear that using AutoPeel helps you to avoid contracting salmonella. It doesn't matter if there are a hundred other ways to avoid salmonella contamination. Your positioning should be that AutoPeel is THE way.

Now that you have developed a creative and comforting brand promise, it is time to destroy the competition with disruptional marketing, the subject of the next chapter.

# CHAPTER 14

# DISRUPTIONAL MARKETING

Astonishing, unbelievable, incredible, surprising, unconventional, delightful, startling! These are just some of the adjectives that should describe your marketing efforts. In contrast, the adjectives used to describe most rust-belt marketing programs typically include the words boring, conventional, predictable, traditional, undifferentiated, same-old, etc.

The reason is that rust-belt companies don't often have much in the way of new products. Rust-belt marketing programs tend to tout the company slogan and not much else. They use what I call "missionary" advertising that brags about how long the company has been in business or how reliable they are. If they do any product marketing at all, they tend to recycle the old products with brand extensions.

They use only two marketing methods—a direct sales force and maybe a few marketing people, in addition to the use of trade publication advertising. I would argue they don't need a sales force at all, only customer service people and order takers. Most rust-belt companies have been around a long time—decades and decades, in fact. Because of that, their customers already know all about them—not much to market here. If your customers already know everything about your product and there is nothing new to tell them, why do you need salespeople? Why would you need any marketing people?

Years ago I took over a failing rust-belt division of a Fortune 500 company. It was an absolute mess. It was an old-line company established over 100 years ago. The market already knew everything there was to know about it, so there was no reason to market anything, and the marketing department was sitting around doing nothing.

When I first sat down with the head of marketing, I asked him why he wasn't finding a creative way to differentiate the company from the competition. I asked him why he continued to place the same old tired ads in the trade publications, and why he kept using the same old tired booth at the trade shows. Moreover, why wasn't he doing anything creative to market the company's products? In short, I asked him why he wasn't doing anything.

Before he answered, he gave me a condescending, "You don't understand, kid" look. What he said astonished me, but proved my point about rust-belt marketing perfectly. He said, "Marketing can't do a thing to affect the price. Marketing can't do a thing to affect promotion. We can't do a thing to increase sales." I guess he missed the three P's of marketing in marketing school. Price, place, and promotion. At the time, I thought he was just an idiot and was too lazy and too caught up in rust-belt speak to do what needed to be done.

Although I didn't realize it at the time, what he told me really was true. Rust-belt marketers really can't do a thing until they are given something new to do something about. So, if you are running a rust-belt company that is not planning cool, new, high-technology products, and you want to cut expenses, the first place you should look is to your marketing budget, as there is no sense in paying them if they can't do anything. Second, you should look to your sales budget. If they are just taking orders from old products, it would be better to pay an order entry clerk and save a lot of expense.

Let's assume you have developed new, high-technology products.

You will need a new marketing approach, as you can't go to market wearing the same old rust-belt marketing clothes you wore with the rust-belt products. If you do, no one will notice it. No one will believe you really do have cool new products. Besides, the market's eyes will glaze over when they see your tired old rust-belt trade publication advertisements, and you will be wasting a lot of money.

Your new marketing approach needs to be fresh, contemporary, and most importantly, "astonishing." You need that to cut through all the noise in the market. You need to cut through all the disbelief from the market that your company isn't rust-belt anymore. You need to counter the claims your competitors will make that they have always been high-technology and you are not. Remember, you will have new competitors in the high-technology world. You are no longer competing against your old friends the rust-belt guys. In fact, you have to ignore your old rust-belt competitors. You don't want to market where they do, and you don't want to advertise where they do—you want to set yourself apart from them.

You need to make this distinction without simply mimicking what your new high-technology competitors are doing. Also, you need to look cooler, more advanced, and more distinctive than they are. Whatever you have been doing does not apply anymore. I know what you have been doing because I used to do it. Full-page, four-color ads in trade publications that convey nothing and result in nothing. Trade shows that have more competitors in your booth than customers—sound familiar?

You need disruptional marketing, and it should focus on three areas:

1. Trade shows
2. Social media
3. Cause marketing

# 1. TRADE SHOWS

Rust-belt marketers all use the same playbook in trade shows: throw up a booth, jam as many products as you can into it, have a few sales guys hang around in case a customer decides to come into it, and then collect business cards for the follow-up. More often than not, they don't have any new products to put in the booth anyway. So why do they waste all that time and money to display products the customers already know all about and are probably already buying anyway? Because that is the way it has always been done. However, here is a dirty little secret: Sales guys like to go to trade shows; moreover, they get to play golf at the show outings and hang out with their buddies in the bars after the show. Lastly, it is a good time for the spouses too.

Just look at any rust-belt trade show booth. Usually, there will be two sales guys standing in front of the booth with arms crossed as if they were guarding the Queen of England, with potential customers nowhere in sight. In fact, anyone walking by the booth cannot even see what is inside because of what I call the "barbarians guarding the gate."

But hey, who cares? You could fire a cannon in most rust-belt trade shows and not hit a single customer. It is more likely you would hit a competitor. Having a booth that looks like Sanford & Son's junkyard is not the answer. Also, having a few sales guys standing around waiting to see their buddies (which are more likely to be competitors than customers) is not the answer either.

You could eliminate the whole trade show expense and spend that money on something else, but that doesn't mean you should. What you should do is restructure the whole process of trade show marketing, which comes in three parts.

### Part One: Marketing before the show.

This is where you need to be very strategic, creative, and contemporary. That means social media. Pound for pound, social media is a lot cheaper than traditional marketing channels. These days, your new customers (high-technology ones) hang out there. Remember, while your old rust-belt customers still hang out in trade publications, the new ones don't. They are younger, digitally-enabled, and better educated.

You need to reach your new customers where they live. That is on Facebook, Instagram, Twitter, and LinkedIn. These places are where you touch them first. The idea is to entice them there to go to your website for more information. The first thing you do is put up a killer website that stands out from the competition. Now is not the time to reach for GoDaddy or have your nephew throw something together for you.

Your website has to be professionally done and maintained. Once you've expended the upfront costs, maintaining it and using it as a marketing communication tool is a whole lot cheaper than trade pub ads. The website needs to be elegant, high-tech, contemporary, easy to navigate, and it should also be trackable. You need to know who was on it, how long they stayed, and what interested them the most. Google Analytics is a great tool for doing this. However, don't try and use it by yourself. Get some professional help from someone who understands the lingo and can make meaning out of the raw data.

To do all of this, you need to hire a digital marketing expert. The print marketing people you have used in rust-belt marketing have probably not upgraded their skills to the digital world. If they have, great. If not, you need to replace them and use that expense for a digital expert. A digital expert can navigate the world of social media marketing. He or she can lead the process of creating a new website, understanding the data it collects, and leading the ongoing process of digital marketing through the social media world.

Once you have your social media assets in place, it could take quite some time before you see the results. If you are patient, over time you will see that these efforts slowly build results over time. Every month, you should review its progress. Are the number of "hits" on your social media climbing or not? If they don't climb you know that you may need to make some adjustments in your approach. My senior leadership team and I do monthly reviews with our digital marketing people.

The questions you should always ask in these reviews, and in all of your marketing efforts, are:

- How are people finding your social media?
- What interested them the most and why?

Once you know how effective your marketing efforts are, you can do more of what works and less of what doesn't. Although it sounds simple, you would be surprised how many marketers don't do this. You should look to consumer advertising for your role models. A perfect example is MyPillow. I once interviewed its CEO, Mike Lindell, for the League of Extraordinary CEOs column that appears regularly in the *American City Business Journals* (http://www.bizjournals.com/bizjournals/bio/18941/Steve+Blue).

Mike Lindell told me that he measures the effectiveness of every ad he places. He gets quite specific about this, even going as far as measuring a one-time slot on a particular television station against another. He does this, like so many other consumer marketers, by using a special offer code. As an example, when he sees the one-time slot drop off, he stops using it and directs the commercials to another time slot that is performing well. This is exactly the approach you need to take in measuring and adjusting your marketing efforts.

***Part Two: What you put into your trade show booth and how you position it.***

There are four golden rules here:

1. Don't ever waste valuable booth space with products that your customers already know all about. If you feel compelled to represent them, don't place the physical product itself. Use a digital image.

2. Don't use old, clunky looking pedestals that the trade show organizer provides to display products. Buy your own and make them acrylic, high-tech looking, and consistent with the look and feel of the product. There is no sense in showing a neural network device on a 1950s-era pedestal that looks like your grandma's couch.

3. Position your new products as close to the front of the booth as the show organizer will allow. I almost always position mine practically in the aisle. It is very difficult to get customers to come into your booth, so make it easy for them to see your new products without entering the booth. If they stop to admire the product, you have a reason to invite them in for more discussion, and they have a reason to want to, which leads to the next point.

4. Often a product is best demonstrated in the field and doesn't show well in a booth. If that is the case, hire a professional to create a virtual or augmented reality demonstration of your product. When the customer can actually "see, feel, and hear the product," it is far more effective than sitting on a pedestal in your booth. Although this is an expensive endeavor, it is well worth it. Depending on how extensive you get, expect to pay $50-100K.

*Part Three: Entice customers to come into your booth.*

Rust-belt marketers spend a ton of money on a big booth filled with junk. A customer couldn't get in there even if they wanted to. The reason why they don't is that it is not a very attractive, comfortable place to be. Here are a few ideas to make it attractive and comfortable.

- If you have ever been to a trade show you know your feet and knees start to ache from walking around on concrete floors. Your customers feel the same way. After a while, all they want to do is walk through it as fast as they can, collect a few brochures, and leave. So make your booth more like an oasis for tired feet than a prison no one wants to enter. As an extra, install nice comfortable directors' chairs in the booth.

- Offer cool refreshments to sip on while they rest their tired feet—and then discuss your products with them.

- Finally, don't just have your barbarian guardians at the gate stand in front of the booth hoping customers enter. Get them! They are all over the exhibit hall! In my company, we have a very attractive and engaging woman ask them to come to our booth. She entices them with a provocative question: "Are you concerned about safety?" Since everyone in the rail industry is, no one says, "No." Now that she has piqued their interest, she brings them to the booth, sits them in the director's chair, and offers them refreshments. Then, she gives them an iPad and Miller Ingenuity branded headphones to view a short video we have prepared to demonstrate our products. A salesman takes over after the video.

*Capturing customer reactions for use later*

Trade shows can be the gift that keeps on giving. You don't have to let them be a single event. Use them again and again in as much marketing media as you can. But how do you do that? Here is what I do. I have a professional videographer standing outside our booth at every trade show. Not only is he an expert in video but he is also a former television personality and interviewer, therefore, he knows how to draw opinions and reactions from people in a non-threatening way.

Once our salesman has finished chatting with the customer about our product, and when they are leaving the booth, that is when my video guy springs into action. He asks permission to film a short interview; then he captures their reaction and opinions about the new products they saw.

In most cases, these interviews are very complimentary and favorable. Then, we package the interviews professionally within our brand, and use them all over social media and in promotional packages for other customers.

## 2. SOCIAL MEDIA

The second major plank in disruptive marketing is the use of social media. Although it was covered in the section detailing how to market the show before the show, I have a few other points you should be aware of.

- Social media is changing and evolving almost every day. Don't get stuck in a rut of using one media (i.e., LinkedIn). As the social media landscape changes, different media will be more or less useful to you. It used to be that LinkedIn was the social media for business people and Facebook was for teenagers. However, this is not so anymore.

- Cover all your social media bases by having an active presence on all of them, making sure to include Facebook, Twitter, and LinkedIn as your primary channels. Tomorrow, "all of them" will probably be one or two more that have not yet emerged.

- Post something frequently on all your social media assets. While nobody knows the algorithms Google's search engine uses, most people agree it looks for frequent postings and activity. These postings should be relevant, useful, interesting, and timely.

  - By relevant, I mean don't just throw out posts for the sake of it. Make sure they are relevant to the market you are targeting. As an example, don't post about lawnmower maintenance in the plumbing market, and for God's sake, don't ever post: "How I spent my summer vacation."

  - Make them as useful as possible. I often post articles I have written in the major business magazines. These are useful "how to" articles that link back to my company.

  - Always make the postings interesting! Remember, "boring is the enemy of breaking through."

  - Post white papers that are written to reinforce your company as technical experts. Just be sure they are useful to the reader. Don't just toot your own horn.

  - Finally, make them timely. Google isn't interested (and neither is your market) in breaking news that broke last month. Once again, this is not a job for your nephew. This is a job for your newly-hired digital marketing expert.

- Video has become the preferred media for the world to receive information. In fact, 300 hours of video are uploaded to YouTube every single minute! Almost *five billion* videos are watched on it *every single day*! You should use video extensively on your social media. Think about it, which would you prefer, to read a long-winded story about something or to watch it on a video? In cases where the video isn't appropriate, use interesting photos.

## 3. CAUSE MARKETING

The third major plank in disruptional marketing is the use of "cause marketing." Cause marketing is when you tie your marketing efforts to a worthwhile cause that your customers care about. Here are some reasons why you should use it.

- In 2015[1], a Cone Communications research study found that 91% of global consumers expect their brands to do more than just make a profit—they expect their brands to be socially responsible.

- A 2014 Nielson study[2] found that 42% of North American shoppers would pay extra for products and services from companies committed to making a positive social impact.

- It is a great way to differentiate yourself from the competition. If you get ahead of this curve by being the first one to use cause marketing, you will have claimed your space in the cause marketing world. Here are a few examples of brands you are familiar with – that are using cause marketing:

  - ➤ Starbucks *Raise A Cup To A Good Cause.* Starbucks donates a certain percentage of sales to selected social causes. Now it is arguable if that drives more sales or not. However, what it does do is create positive awareness for the brand.

  - ➤ Jet Blue's *Soar with Reading.* It has partnered with Random House to provide children in low-income neighborhoods free books. Does this increase Jet Blue sales? Who knows, but it undeniably creates positive awareness for the brand. Heaven knows, airlines need as much positive publicity as they can get.

> ➤ *UberGiving* is a program where people can request an Uber car to pick up clothing and food donations for distribution to local charity partners. Uber needs the positive publicity this program provides. But it also gets more engagement on their app from it, which probably drives more sales, but certainly, drives more awareness of the brand.

> ➤ Pet Smart donates food to a pet in need for every bag of food they sell. Is it possible a consumer will choose Pet Smart over another brand for that reason alone? Why wouldn't that consumer just donate food to a pet in need and then buy a brand other than Pet Smart? Because that would require two decisions and two actions: buying the food and finding a charity to donate to. Simply buying Pet Smart does it all in one move.

> ➤ One other example is Hellman's mayonnaise. It touts that it now sources its oils "responsibly" and in "environmentally sensitive" ways. I have no idea what that means, but to some people, it comforts them to know that. That is a perfect example of differentiation in an undifferentiated product. After all, can you tell the difference between Hellman's and a generic brand?

I am not suggesting you spend more marketing dollars to include cause marketing expense. You probably can't afford that. What I am suggesting is to divert some of your existing marketing expenses to cause marketing. This is not a permanent requirement, as in all marketing expenses, you should try it for a year and then measure the results.

You might skip a few full-page, four-color "we are the best" trade publication advertisements and funnel that money into a cause marketing campaign. After all, no one ever believes your claims to "be the best," but they might believe it if you actually do something, like investing in a cause, to prove that you are.

In the final chapter, an 18th Century Prussian general has some words of advice for you.

**Chapter Bibliography**
1. 2015 Cone Communications/Ebiquity Global CSR Study. http://www.conecomm.com/research-blog/2015-cone-communications-ebiquity-global-csr-study. (Extracted 8/15/17.)

2. Nielsen Global Survey on Social Responsibility. *Global Consumers are Willing to Put Their Money Where Their Heart is When it Comes to Goods and Services from Companies Committed to Social Responsibility.* June 17, 2014.
http://www.nielsen.com/us/en/press-room/2014/global-consumers-are-willing-to-put-their-money-where-their-heart-is.html. (Extracted 8/15/17.)

# CHAPTER 15

# THE FOG OF WAR

When you start down your metamorphosis, you should have an endgame in mind. For example, what markets do you expect to introduce it in? Which customers will you target first? How will you use creative marketing and branding to position the company and the products in the new world of high-technology? All these decisions need to be made well in advance.

Still. . . most of those decisions will be useless. Most of the assumptions you make will be wrong. Most of the plans you make will go up in smoke. You have to be ready for that. You need to think like Carl von Clausewitz.

Carl von Clausewitz was a 18th Century Prussian general best known for his thinking and critical examination of all aspects of war. His most relevant and famous work was *On War*, which is still studied by military tacticians to this day and contains his famous quote: "No campaign plan survives the first encounter with the enemy." He further noted that "unexpected developments unfolding in the fog of war called for rapid decisions by alert commanders."

When you enter the combat arena of the high-technology world, the market will be enveloped by fog, just like the fog of war. You will face uncertainty and ambiguity as your market and high-technology products unfold. The answers will not be clear, and market conditions will change before you can release your new products for commercialization. The competition will make moves that you didn't expect or anticipate, and your customers will do things that are inconvenient and not particularly helpful. The technology you are developing will most likely take a number of years. As many unforeseen events will happen on your battlefield during that time, you will need to be an alert commander and be prepared for rapid decisions. Further, you need to be able to turn on a dime.

It is comparable to a football game. After the snap, nobody knows what will happen next – despite discussing a plan beforehand. Every player knows what he is supposed to do and what is supposed to happen, but sometimes it happens according to the playbook while other times it doesn't. No one knows how it will turn out until the play is over. That is the way your market works. That is how your planning will unfold. You won't know how it will turn out until it is over.

Sometimes you will be pleasantly surprised that the outcome was right on target, maybe even better than you expected. However, more often than not, the outcome will be worse than you expected. So, the importance here is on being an alert commander and making rapid decisions.

However, an "alert commander" cannot be an armchair general. You have to get out of your corner office and get into the battlefield. Clausewitz teaches us that we face "incomplete, dubious, and often erroneous information." That is the best case scenario. It gets worse if you are getting second- and third-hand information from the field. This is why you need to be the one on the battlefield. You want to see and hear firsthand what is happening.

**You need to "feel" the tempo, the pace, and the reactions of customers.**

When you first introduce a new product to a customer, they will either work to qualify or disqualify it. If they like it, they will help you. They will find a way to get it qualified, and if they don't, they will scuttle you and find a reason to disqualify it. You cannot know which it is unless you see and feel their reactions up close and personal. Hence, you need to see their faces by asking them questions and noting how they react. However, bear in mind that they will often not tell you how they feel about the product because most buyers play their cards close to the chest, so you have to spend time with them to know for sure.

You should view your markets as a battlefield, as the conditions are constantly changing, especially in high-technology markets. The ink won't be dry on your plans before you have to change them, so always be ready to change them.

# AFTERWORD

There is a Chinese story of a farmer who used an old horse to till his fields. One day, the horse escaped into the hills, and when the farmer's neighbors sympathized with the old man over his bad luck, the farmer replied, "Bad luck? Good luck? Who knows?" A week later, the horse returned with a herd of horses from the hills and this time the neighbors congratulated the farmer on his good luck. His reply was, "Good luck? Bad luck? Who knows?"

Then, when the farmer's son was attempting to tame one of the wild horses, he fell off its back and broke his leg. Everyone thought this was very bad luck, except for the farmer, whose only reaction was, "Bad luck? Good luck? Who knows?"

Some weeks later, the army marched into the village and conscripted every able-bodied youth they found there. When they saw the farmer's son with his broken leg, they let him off. Now was that good luck or bad luck?

Who knows?

This is what your metamorphosis will be like. It will be full of good luck and bad luck. You won't know until it plays out later. Bad things will happen that turn out to be good, and good things will happen that turn out to be bad. I still remember getting the first really big deal for my first high-tech product—only to lose it all because the customer shuffled the top guys out and brought new guys in who didn't like the product.

At the time, that sure seemed like bad luck, however, that shuffle lead me to pivot the product into another market, which was ultimately a better market to be in.

Your journey will be more like a start-up than the established, legacy business you are used to running. You have to treat that part of it as if it were a start-up. However, at the same time, you have to run the legacy business in the traditional way you always have. It would be a mistake to try and manage both sides of the business the same way. Since you already know how to run the legacy business, I won't take the time to discuss that here. However, let's look at how you need to run the start-up.

A start-up is almost always cash-starved. Therefore, it has to earn its cash by demonstrating to its investors that it is making progress that is worthy of more investment. This is how you should view your start-up—make it earn its way and prove its worth before you plow more money into it. Bootstrap it along by spending a little money and see how it goes; if it goes well, spend a little more.

Start-ups value creativity and flat hierarchies. They have very few policies and procedures, and moreover, they make it up as they go along. In light of this, don't let your start-up become saddled with the policies and procedures in place with your legacy business, as this would only slow it down and stifle creativity. On the other hand, your legacy business values stability and predictability. This comes from those policies and procedures, so don't try and run it without them, which would cause chaos—keep the two separate.

Some people have asked me, "but wouldn't I want the legacy business to be more like the start-up?" The short answer is no, at least not in the short run. It is crucial to keep the legacy business paying the bills until the start-up starts to earn its keep. Over the long run, the start-up will morph into the new legacy business as the old legacy business slowly dies out. Let that happen naturally, in its own time.

Leading a start-up and a legacy business requires two different mindsets and styles—you'll need both. This is the dichotomy you will face in your metamorphosis.

One final word. When you embark on your metamorphosis, you will need to be bold. Only time will tell you whether you will be considered a bold visionary or a fool.

Does fortune favor the bold or the foolish?

Who knows?

## About Steven

Steven L. Blue is an internationally-recognized expert on leading change and business transformation. He shows companies how to triple and even quadruple growth. Steve regularly contributes to leading media and industry outlets, such as *FOX, BusinessWeek, Forbes, Inc., The Huffington Post, Entrepreneur Magazine, AMA, Europe Business Review, The Adam Carolla Show*, and *The Wall Street Journal*. His insights have led many media outlets to refer to him as America's leading Mid-Market CEO.

Steve is the President and CEO of Miller Ingenuity—an innovative company revolutionizing traditional safety solutions for railway workers. Its products protect assets, preserve the environment, and save lives. Steve also serves on a variety of boards in safety, banking, healthcare, and university business schools, and is the first CEO-in-Residence for the College of Business at Winona State University.

Steve is also a best-selling author of four critically-acclaimed books that target executives, leaders, entrepreneurs, and anyone seeking to learn the secrets of success in the corporate world. His third book, *American Manufacturing 2.0: What Went Wrong and How to Make It Right*, was published in 2016 and offers an in-depth take on American manufacturing, inspirational success stories, and a guide on how to regain the key position America once held in the manufacturing industry. Steve's additional books include *The Ten Million Dollar Employee: When Your Most Toxic Liability Meets Your Most Important Customer*, and *Burnarounds: Unlocking the Double-Digit Profit Code*.

Steve's fourth book, *Mastering the Art of Success* became a best seller its second day in publication. He co-authored this book with Jack Canfield (*Chicken Soup for the Soul* series). In his book, he describes how any company can unleash its Innovational Potential™. This book earned him the prestigious Quilly® Award and induction into the National Academy of Best-Selling Authors®.

Steve is a business movie producer. His latest film, *Getting Everything You Can Out of All You've Got: The Jay Abraham Story*, chronicles the life and times of this legendary marketing genius.

His 7 Values of Ingenuity® is the preeminent system to achieve exponential growth in a business. His Innovational Potential™ offers a roadmap of how any company can ignite its creativity and innovation capability.

Steve holds a Bachelor's Degree from the State University of New York and an MBA from Regis University.

You can connect with Steve at:

- www.StevenLBlue.com
- Facebook: fb.me/StevenLBlue
- Twitter: @StevenLBlue
- LinkedIn.com/in/stevenblue